CHANGES AND CHOICES
WITH ARTICLES FROM THE NEW YORK TIMES

現代諸相 ニューヨークタイムズ

Edited with Notes and Exercises
by
Rume KITA
and
Keith Wesley ADAMS

EIHŌSHA

Copyright © THE NEW YORK TIMES COMPANY.
Permission granted by The New York Times Licensing Group through
Japan Uni Agency, Inc., Tokyo.

はじめに

　ニューヨークタイムズを読んで世界の現状を知る読解用テキストをお届けします．
　今回は7編の記事を半期用テキストとして編集し，4つのカテゴリーに分けました．

　I. Lifestyle Choices: 昨今の私たちのライフスタイルは実に多様化しています．たとえば食生活です．健康のため，あるいは宗教や信念に従って私たちは様々な食生活を選べる世の中に生きていますが，Unit 1 ではペットの食事にもそれが反映している様子がわかります．

　II. Evolving Languages: 言語の変化に目を向けてみましょう．Unit 2 ではアフリカで使われているフランス語の現状が描かれます．公用語のフランス語が地元の言語や英語と混じり合って変容することはもはや止められないようです．Unit 3 はスペイン語についてです．文法上，男性形・女性形を有する言語がジェンダーニュートラルな方向に変化するのは今や必然とも言えるかもしれません．

　III. Nature and Humanity: a Complex Relationship: 自然と人間の暮らしを考えるカテゴリーです．Unit 4 には気候変動の厳しさが映し出されています．暑すぎる夏に日常生活を脅かされた経験が皆さんもきっとあることでしょう．暑さが身体や生活スタイルに及ぼす影響を読みましょう．Unit 5 はコロナ禍が自然に及ぼした影響についてです．人間の活動が大幅に停止したときに自然界ではどのようなことが起こったのか．期せずして壮大な実験のチャンスとなったコロナ禍のその結果を見てみましょう．

　IV. Trying to Lessen Our Footprint: 日常生活を営む上での環境負荷について考えたことはあるでしょうか．Unit 6 で読むのは食品廃棄物の問題です．飽食の時代の今，日々の食事で必ず出る残飯をどう処理すれば良いのか，この記事がヒントになるでしょう．Unit 7 は，今や何にでも使われる石油由来の製品やプラスティックについての考察です．環境に影響するプラスティック製品を使わずして私たちの生活は成り立つでしょうか．賢明な対応の仕方はあるのでしょうか．

　各ユニットには，記事の前後に練習問題を配置しています．Pre-reading には，記事に出てくる英単語を使ったクロスワード，記事をより身近に捉えることを狙いとしたディスカッション，内容に関連したグラフや地図の読み取りがあります．Post-reading には，記事に出てきた語句の復習問題，内容の理解度をチェックするための英問英答，そして，記事の中身をより発展的に考えるためのリサーチ課題を置きました．
　今回の企画も，膨大な数のニューヨークタイムズの記事の中から，大学生の皆さんが読むにふさわしいものを集めるところからスタートしました．一過性の話題ではないこと，長さが適切であること，理論ばかりでなく情景が思い浮かぶような例が紹介され

ていることなどを念頭に置いて選びました．Pre-reading と Post-reading は長くこの企画を共にしている Keith Wesley Adams 氏の手によるものです．記事の本質を見極めたディスカッションなど，良い課題を考えてくださいました．

　最後になりますが，今回の企画を応援してくださった英宝社の佐々木元氏，そして編集段階で支えてくださった佐藤貴博氏に心より御礼申し上げます．

2024年　夏

喜多　留女

Preface - Changes and Choices
Keith Wesley Adams

    Our world is changing faster than anytime in human history. The changes affect every aspect of our lives: our bodies and minds, our language, our relationships with each other and even our pets, but most of all, our environment. Some of these changes are based on conscious choices and some are unconscious. Some of these changes may seem unnecessary, even a little crazy, others highly necessary and the only intelligent thing to do. Some of the changes will affect us in a clear and positive manner, and others in uncertain and potentially dangerous ways. What is certain is that most of these changes are based on our own choices and actions. We now live in the Anthropocene era, an era in which for the first time in the history of our planet, humans are the greatest actors of change in the world. The effects of our choices today will be long lasting, some even permanent, so we had better choose wisely. Without conscious and intelligent choices we may condemn ourselves, and our civilization, as well as millions of species to extinction. Let us choose wisely and make the choices and changes that are needed to survive and live without misery.

    This book looks at a few of the choices people are purposefully making and some of the changes that are happening regardless of our conscious selection. As these are all global issues, the texts relate stories from countries around the world: the United States, Ivory Coast, Spain, Iraq, and South Korea. Section I looks at changes and choices people are making concerning relationships with our pets (Unit 1). Section II looks at how languages are changing both consciously and unconsciously through globalization and as colonial legacy (Unit 2), and how some people are trying to stop the changes (Unit 3). Section III focuses on our environment, how having changed nature, it will force us to change the way we live (Unit 4). We also look at how nature reacts in the absence of humans thanks to observations during covid, and how humans sometimes benefit nature (Unit 5). Finally in section IV, we look at both successful and unsuccessful conscious attempts to improve our relationship with nature (Units 6 & 7).

    This is now our 6th textbook in this series. As always, my colleague Rume Kita, has chosen and edited the articles, made all the necessary translations and explanations into Japanese. As usual, I have provided the various cross words, word matches, research and discussion questions. However, it is Rume Kita who checks, corrects and suggests the necessary changes. Together we discuss titles, organization, ideas and make our final decisions. We hope you enjoy this volume in our now almost 20 year series. May we choose the changes that will help all of us, all nations, races, cultures and other species thrive and survive.

Sincerely,
Keith Adams,

◆ CONTENTS ◆

I. Lifestyle Choices
Unit 1   Giving Our Pets Meals for People 4
　　　　菜食？それともグルテンフリー？ペットの正しい食事法

II. Evolving Languages
Unit 2   The Evolution of French Goes Through Africa 14
　　　　コートジボアール発：アフリカで変容するフランス語

Unit 3   Gender Neutral? A Debate Over Spanish Words 26
　　　　アルゼンチン発：スペイン語はジェンダーニュートラルへ

III. Nature and Humanity: a Complex Relationship
Unit 4   Extreme Heat Will Change Us 36
　　　　危険な暑さ——気候変動の真実

Unit 5   Pandemic Lockdown Healed and Hurt Nature 46
　　　　善か悪か——生態系における人間の役割とは

IV. Trying to Lessen Our Footprint
Unit 6   South Korea Turns Scraps Into Energy 56
　　　　韓国発：食品廃棄物の行方

Unit 7   My Frustrating Attempt At a Plastic-Free Day 66
　　　　プラスチックに触れずに過ごす一日

Changes and Choices
with articles from The New York Times

I

Lifestyle Choices

Unit 1
Giving Our Pets Meals for People

Pre-reading

A: Crossword

Match the words in the Word Bank to their descriptions to fill in the crossword.

Word Bank

Antibiotic-resistant*	Capitalize	Classist	Detrimental	Distrust
Manipulative	Misinformation	Persuaded	Probiotic	Regimen
Seasoned	Skyrocketed	Spawned	Spurred	Supplements
Vegan	Veterinarian	Vetted		

*Use hyphen when filling in the crossword.

Across
1. (v.) Past participle. To give food more flavor by adding spices or savory ingredients.
4. (v.) Simple past. To encourage or inspire someone to a belief or action by argument.
6. (v) Simple past. Rise very rapidly in number.
9. (n.) A person who does not eat meat or any animal by-products such as milk or honey.
10. (v.) Past participle. Evaluated and corrected.
11. (v.) Simple past. To urge or incite to action.
12. (adj.) Beneficial to the upper, but not the lower levels of society.
13. (n.) A specific plan designed to improve or maintain the health of a patient. A regular course of action.
14. (adj.) Intent to control or influence others in a clever and often unfair or selfish way.
15. (n.) Incorrect or misleading written or spoken knowledge.
16. (adj.) Not able to be easily killed by medicine that kills microorganisms.

Down
1. (n.) Something added to enhance a diet to fulfill nutrient requirements.
2. (v.) To turn something to an advantage.
3. (n.) A doctor for animals.
5. (n.) A microorganism that restores or maintains good bacteria to the digestive tract.
6. (v.) Past participle. To create, give birth.
7. (adj.) Harmful or damaging.
8. (n.) Not have confidence in. A sense of not being able to rely on another.

B: Discussion Questions
1. Have you ever owned a pet? What kind of pet was it?
2. What did you feed it? Was it healthy?
3. Have you ever been on a diet? What kind of diet? Did it work?
4. Did you ever put your pet on a diet?
5. Would you ever give a pet the same diet as yourself?
6. What do you think is healthy eating for dogs or cats?

C: Reading Graphs, Maps and Statistics

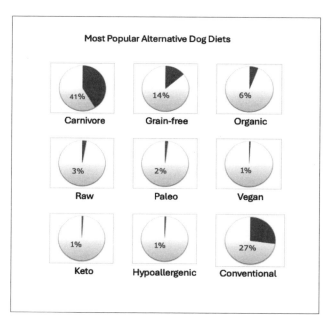

1. Look up the meaning of
Carnivore:
Organic:
Paleo:
Vegan:
Keto:
Hypoallergenic:
Conventional:

https://www.lemonade.com/pet/explained/deep-dive-into-dog-diets/ をもとに編注者が作成

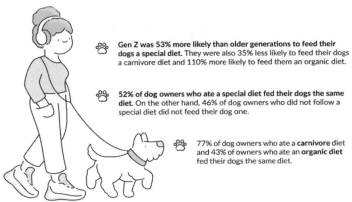

Gen Z was 53% more likely than older generations to feed their dogs a special diet. They were also 35% less likely to feed their dogs a carnivore diet and 110% more likely to feed them an organic diet.

52% of dog owners who ate a special diet fed their dogs the same diet. On the other hand, 46% of dog owners who did not follow a special diet did not feed their dog one.

77% of dog owners who ate a carnivore diet and 43% of owners who ate an organic diet fed their dogs the same diet.

https://www.lemonade.com/pet/explained/deep-dive-into-dog-diets/

2. Which generation is most likely to give their dogs a special diet?
3. What percentage of people who ate a special diet gave their dogs the same one?

Number of dogs, cats and pets by country.

Country	Dog Population	Cat Population	Bird Population	Aquaria Population	Small Mammal Population
United States	69,929,000	74,059,000	8,300,000		
China	27,400,000	53,100,000			
United Kingdom	13,000,000	12,000,000	1,600,000	8,000,000	
Japan	12,000,000	7,300,000			
Philippines	11,600,000				
Germany	10,600,000	15,200,000	4,900,000	2,300,000	4,900,000
India	10,200,000				
Spain	9,313,000	5,859,000	6,991,000	691,000	1,523,000
Argentina	9,200,000	3,000,000			
Italy	8,755,000	10,228,000	12,882,000	1,500,000	1,816,000
Poland	8,019,000	7,125,000	1,144,000	380,000	1,217,000
France	7,600,000	14,900,000	5,800,000	1,252,000	2,800,000

4. Based on the chart, name 3 countries which prefer dogs to cats, and three which prefer cats to dogs.

https://worldpopulationreview.com/country-rankings/pet-ownership-statistics-by-country

Amount of money spent on a dog in the U.S. by State each year.

https://mosquitojoe.com/blog/states-that-spend-the-most-on-their-pets/

5. Based on the map, which State in the U.S. is most likely to spend money on special diets for their dogs?

By Priya Krishna Feb. 22, 2022

Karl Malone starts his day with a breakfast that includes ashwagandha root and psyllium husk powder. His dinner is always seasoned with ground turmeric, and then he takes his joint supplements. He goes on two brisk walks daily and avoids restaurant food, as his doctor recommended he lose weight.

Karl Malone is a dog — an 11-year-old sandy-brown Australian shepherd mix.

Darshna Shah, Mr. Malone's owner, believes that this regimen — a blend of advice from friends, her veterinarian and pet newsletters, and nutritional remedies her family grew up with in India — has greatly improved her companion's health.

Ms. Shah, 64, a former insurance executive in Cerritos, Calif., used to think that if her pets were housed and well fed, they would be fine. But the increasing focus on wellness persuaded her to do more. "Their quality of life depends on their health."

The rate of pet adoptions in the United States, spurred by the pandemic, skyrocketed in 2021 to a six-year high, while human birthrates have steadily declined. As people reimagine what parenthood can look like, pet owners are devoting considerable thought and money to what their dogs, cats, hamsters, goldfish and other animals eat.

For many owners, the answer is customizing their pets' diets to match their own eating habits.

There are pets on raw-food diets, gluten-free diets, grain-free diets, vegan and vegetarian diets. There are pets that munch on treats flavored like a turmeric latte or made with CBD, pets that never skip a probiotic or vitamin C supplement. Some owners whip up special menus at home, while others shop for the growing number of products tailored to these diets.

Oscar, a terrier-Chihuahua mix living in New York, is vegetarian, just like his owner, Roopa Kalyanaraman Marcello, 42, a public-health policy specialist who feeds the dog store-bought vegetarian pet food.

"He is part of our family," Ms. Marcello said. "It would be weird to me if one of my kids started eating meat."

Last year, Jennifer Donald, who teaches criminal justice at the University of Maryland, suspected that the wheat-filled kibble she fed to her Labrador retriever, Moses, was responsible for his digestive issues.

Ms. Donald, 52, has celiac disease and does not eat gluten. She

1	wild-caught	「天然の」
3	grain bowl	「グレインボウル」→ Note 2
5	the U. S. Food and Drug Administration	「米国食品医薬品局」
9	lag behind	「遅れをとる」
10	brim with ~	「~で溢れている」
11	be up to ~	「~次第である」
13	the American Kennel Club	アメリカの愛犬家団体
17	fad diet	「一時的な流行の食餌法」
19	generalization	「一般法則化」
27	subset	「一派, 小さなグループ」
28	influencer	「インフルエンサー」影響力を持つ情報発信者のこと
37	be in one's best interest	「~のためになる」

recently adopted the same diet for Moses, feeding him wild-caught salmon, sweet potatoes, boiled eggs, coconut oil and rice — the same ingredients she uses to make grain bowls for herself and her husband.

There are no clear or simple rules for how to feed a pet. The U. S. Food and Drug Administration has cautioned about certain animal diets and regulates how pet food is manufactured and labeled, but offers much vaguer guidance on the ingredients. Veterinarians have differing opinions, and scientific research on pet health lags behind studies on humans. The internet is brimming with advice, and misinformation. It's primarily up to owners to decide whom to trust.

The American Kennel Club, a registry for dogs, provides online educational materials and recommendations about diet, all vetted by its chief veterinary officer. So it dismays Brandi Hunter Munden, the organization's vice president of communications, to see people turn to fad diets that can pose the same hazards for pets as for humans.

They can perpetuate generalizations about health, she said, promote regimens that aren't backed by research and capitalize on people's anxieties about not doing enough for their animals.

The market for what the pet-food industry calls "nutritious pet food" — higher-priced products that claim to contain premium or nutritionally enhanced ingredients — is expected to reach $17.9 billion by 2026, according to a report last year by Pet Insight, an analytics company. Pet wellness in general has become an even bigger industry, and has spawned a subset of social media influencers and Facebook groups devoted to refining the diets of all kinds of animals.

The intense focus on what pets eat is tied to the increased time owners have spent at home with their pets during the pandemic, when many people became more mindful of their own health, said Ms. Hunter Munden, the Kennel Club executive.

But imposing a new lifestyle on a loved one can become fraught when the beneficiary isn't able to communicate — or make its own decisions, she said. "Dogs will eat anything you put in front of them, but it is not necessarily in their best interests."

In 1999, the human and animal nutritionist Kymythy Schultze, 63, self-published a book on raw pet food called "The Ultimate Diet: Natural Nutrition for Dogs and Cats." She had started feeding her pets that way after eliminating processed food from her own diet to alleviate health problems. The premise is similar to that of the Paleo diet: that people should eat the way their ancestors did during the Stone Age.

Many readers found her recommendations too extreme. Veterinarians, she said, told her that pets couldn't survive on anything but canned or bagged food. "How did cats and dogs thrive for thousand and thousands of years?" said Ms. Schultze. "The stuff in bags and cans hasn't been around very long."

The book has sold tens of thousands of copies. And raw feeding — which includes vegetables, animal proteins, bones and other uncooked ingredients — has gone from fringe to trendy, even though numerous authorities have warned against it.

Conversations about pet diets thrive online, where many owners have grown sizable followings by posting videos of themselves feeding their pets.

Luke Hagopian, 21, has 3.6 million TikTok followers who watch him feed his 45 or so goldfish frozen bloodworms, boiled spinach and boiled cucumber — ideas he picked up from talking to other fish owners online, and from reading websites like wikiHow. He also fields questions about fish diets — even though, he admitted, he is not a medical expert.

Notions of expertise in the pet-health field are changing, and embedded in many owners' interest in wellness is a growing distrust of veterinarians.

When her veterinarian wasn't supportive of a raw diet, Kayla Kowalski, a 21-year-old dog owner, switched to a holistic veterinarian who was. (Holistic veterinarians often combine practices like acupuncture and homeopathy with Western medicine.)

Haley Totes started adding fresh foods like bone broth, beef short ribs, green beans and kefir to her dogs' diets after seeing a TikTok of someone listing the processed ingredients in pet food and reading about diets online. "Some vets are wary of raw, even homemade," she said.

Veterinarians, in turn, become frustrated when people are more willing to believe social media posts than medical professionals.

"Owners trust us enough to make recommendations about their pets' health in areas of like, 'Your pet has a mass we need to remove it and do a biopsy,'" said Dr. Marcus Dela Cruz, a veterinarian in San Luis Obispo, Calif. "But when we make recommendations about food, owners don't feel the same way."

Online misinformation about pet health is rampant, he said, and animals are suffering because of it: Raw meats can carry antibiotic-resistant bacteria, and homemade meals can lack essential nutrients. Vegetarian diets, he said, are not suitable for cats because they need animal protein.

For all the pet owners who believe they've found the key to improving their animals' health with these diets, there are others who feel confused and frustrated by them.

Yishian Yao, 30, who runs an animal care business in El Cerrito, Calif., said pet wellness culture can feel not only classist, as many owners can't afford to buy their animals fresh food and supplements, but also manipulative.

The messaging is, she said, "if you don't do this for the health of your pet, you are not as good a pet parent."

She wondered if the popular belief that pets are like family has actually been detrimental to animals by "putting a human value lens on their food," she said.

"It's not that I don't think pets should be treated and cared for like family," she said. "It is when we equate them to being human when they are not. Is it really what's best for them?"

13 manipulative 「人を巧みに操る」

Notes

1 アメリカでは，劣悪な環境でペットを繁殖させて売買することを防ぐため，多くの州でペットショップでのペット販売が禁止されている．犬や猫を飼う場合は保護施設に出向いて「里親」としてペットを引き取ることが多い．

2 グレインボウルとは，玄米などを中心に野菜や豆を使ったサラダふうの食べ物で，人によって様々にアレンジされる．身体に良いとされる食材を使い，たっぷりとした大きな器で食べることが多い．

3 パレオダイエットとは，農耕や牧畜が発達する以前の旧石器時代の狩猟採取型の食生活を手本とする食事法のこと．野草，根菜，木の実，キノコ，野生動物，魚，昆虫など自然界から容易に入手できるもので食生活を賄う．

4 ホリスティック医学は，身体の調子の悪い部分だけを取り上げて治療するのではなく，身体全体を包括的にとらえる考え方の医療法．自己治癒力を土台とし，西洋医学の利点を生かしながらも，中国やインドなどの伝統医学や栄養療法，心理療法，運動療法などさまざまな代替療法を組み合わせた医療が実践される．

5 ホメオパシーとは，自然治癒力に働きかける代替医療のひとつで，レメディと呼ばれるホメオパシー薬が用いられる．ある病気や症状を引き起こす物質（レメディ）を故意に患者に与えることで，その病気や症状を改善するという「同種療法，同毒療法」である．日本では，安全性や有効性に関するエビデンスは確立されておらず，治療効果も認められていない．

Post-reading

A: Word Match

Write the appropriate description letter in the empty column next to the compounds.

1. Ashwaganda root		a.	Internet stars whose opinions and views and likes inspire thousands to millions of people.
2. Psyllium husk		b.	Part of the Plantago family, the fiber of this plant is good for digestion and heart health.
3. Nutritional remedies		c.	Goods manufactured for a specific group of people.
4. Pet adoptions		d.	An eating regimen that avoids carbohydrates and other proteins that are found in wheat etc.
5. Raw-food		e.	Problems with the processing of foods resulting in various physical ailments such as constipation and diarrhea.
6. Grain/Gluten-free diets		f.	The preventive medical practice of ensuring patients get enough minerals and protein and vitamins throughout their diets.
7. Media influencers		g.	To pass on vague ideas about an issue that may or may not be helpful.
8. Tailored products		h.	Uncooked meals.
9. Criminal justice		i.	To encourage people to follow certain diets.
10. Digestive issues		j.	The underground part of the plant also known as Indian Ginseng, Winter Cherry. Grown in India, it is known for its ability to reduce stress, improve muscle strength, boost cognitive ability and help sleep.
11. Promote regimens		k.	The legal branch that focuses on lawbreakers.
12. Perpetuate generalizations		l.	The taking into the family of a dog or cat to care for.

B: Comprehension Questions

1. Why is it surprising that Karl Malone avoids restaurant food, and starts his day with a special diet of ashwagandha root, psyllium husk, turmeric and joint supplements in order to lose weight?
2. Where did Karl's owner get the idea for this dog food regimen?
3. What spurred the rate of pet adoptions in 2021 to skyrocket?
4. What is the answer for many pet owners to their pet's diet?
5. What different kinds of diets are people feeding their pets?
6. What are the rules concerning feeding pets?
7. Why can't pet owners rely on veterinarians and scientific research for advice on pet food?
8. How much is it expected for the pet food industry to capitalize on people's anxieties about their animals health?
9. What is the Paleo diet, and why did Kymythy Schultze argue dogs do not need canned or bagged food?

10. What does Luke Hagopian show himself feeding his gold fish on TikTok to his 3.6 million followers?
11. Why are veterinarians frustrated?
12. Why does Yishian Yao think wellness culture is classist?

C: Discussion Questions
1. Do you think it is healthy for pets to eat the same food as humans?
2. Why might it not be?
3. Do you think it is good to treat pets as family and/or equate them with humans?
4. Have you ever been to a pet café? What was your experience? What do you think about animals in restaurants?
5. What do you think of the Paleo diet, in which people eat fish, meat, nuts, berries and wild vegetables like our ancestors did over 10,000 years ago?
6. Are their any other diets you would like to or definitely would not like to try? Why?
7. Do you think it is good for people to have pets? Why? What are the benefits and problems?
8. Do you think it is good for animals to be pets? Why/why not?

D: Research Activities
1. Look up the number of dog, cat and other common pet owners around the world.
2. Which country has the most dogs? Cats? Birds?
3. Which country spends the most on pets in the world?
4. How many cats and dogs and other pets are in your country?
5. Which pets are favored in your country, cats or dogs?
6. How much is spent on health care in your country for pets?
7. How much is spent on human health care?

II

Evolving Languages

Unit 2
The Evolution of French Goes Through Africa

Pre-reading

A: Crossword

Match the words in the Word Bank to their descriptions to fill in the crossword.

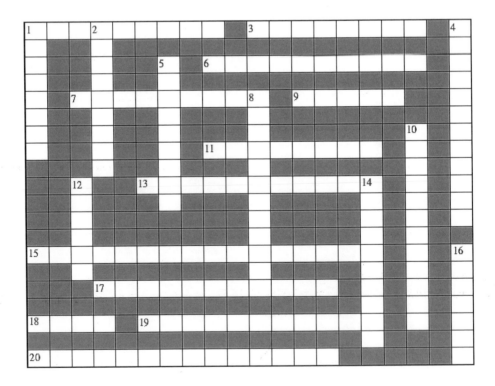

Word Bank

Academician	Ambassadors	Angst	Creolized	Colonized	Decentralization
Democratized	Demographer	Evicted	Flourish	Imitations	Improvisations
Influence	Infusing	Jibe	Legacy	Literally	Proliferated
Protectorate	Resentment	Vitality			

—14—

Across

1. (n.) The act or power of producing an effect without obvious exertion.
3. (n.) Full of life.
6. (n.) Copies, faking the style of the original.
7. (adj.) To pidginize, turn a word of one language into a term in a language of a different community or culture.
9. (n.) A feeling of fear or insecurity.
11. (v.) To grow luxuriantly, thrive, prosper.
13. (n.) A person who studies human populations.
15. (n.) The spreading or distribution of power or people or language from a central authority to regional areas.
17. (n.) Official envoys or representatives of another country.
18. (n.) A short insulting joke.
19. (n.) Professor or one who works in a university concerning themselves with rigorous study.
20. (n.) The act of making up or inventing words, actions and ideas or plans on the spot.

Down

1. (v.) Present participle. To fill with, permeate.
2. (adv.) With exact equivalence. Strict and complete accuracy.
4. (v.) Simple past. To grow by a rapid increase of new parts.
5. (v.) Simple past. To take over and control a people or nation.
8. (v.) Past participle. Make something less authoritarian with more control given to the people.
10. (n.) A political unit or territory dependent on a more powerful state.
12. (n.) Leftover things, policies, and/or structures from an earlier time or in this case government.
14. (n.) A feeling of indignant displeasure, of being wronged, insulted or injured.
16. (v.) Past participle. To be kicked out.

B: Discussion Questions

1. How many different dialogues are there in your language?
2. What are the differences between Osaka-ben and Tokyo dialects?
3. Did you ever make up a new word with your friends in high school?
4. What are some English words you use in Japanese?
5. Do any of them have a different meaning than the original English meaning?
6. A decade ago French used to be about the 14th most spoken Language in the world. Now it is the 5th. Why do you think this is happening?

C: Reading Graphs, Maps and Statistics

SINGLISH	*ENGLISH*
Can lah	Yes
Can leh	Yes, of course
Can lor	Yes, I think so
Can hah?	Are you sure?
Can hor?	Are you sure then?
Can meh?	Are you certain?
Can bo?	Can or not?
Can can	Confirm
Can gua	Maybe
Can liao	Already can / Done
Can wor	Yeah
Can liao la!	OK, enough!

https://www.memrise.com/blog/english-around-the-world

1. Have you heard of Singlish? What country is it from?
2. What does the word "Can" mean? What language is it from?

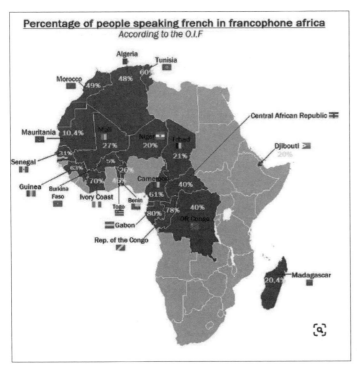

3. Which African country has the largest percentage of French speakers?
4. Which has the least?
5. Name the 3 French speaking North African countries.

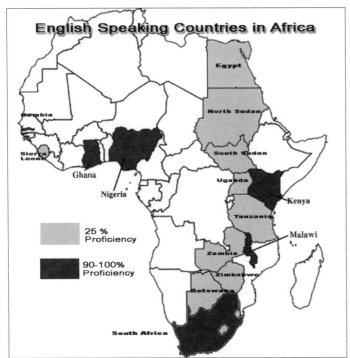

6. Look at both the maps.
   Why do you think English or French are spoken in these countries?
7. Do you think the English spoken in all these countries is the same?

By Elian Peltier Dec. 12, 2023

ABIDJAN, Ivory Coast — French, the world's fifth most spoken language, is changing — perhaps not in the gilded hallways of the institution in Paris that publishes its official dictionary, but on a rooftop in Abidjan, the largest city in Ivory Coast.

There one afternoon, a 19-year-old rapper with the stage name "Marla" rehearsed her upcoming show, surrounded by friends. Her words were mostly French, but the Ivorian slang and English words that she mixed in made a new language.

To speak only French, "c'est zogo" — "it's uncool," said Marla, whose real name is Mariam Dosso, combining a French word with Ivorian slang. But playing with words and languages, she said, is "choco," an abbreviation for chocolate meaning "sweet" or "stylish."

A growing number of words and expressions from Africa are now infusing the French language, spurred by booming populations of young people in West and Central Africa.

More than 60 percent of those who speak French daily now live in Africa, and 80 percent of children studying in French are in Africa. There are as many French speakers in Kinshasa, the capital of the Democratic Republic of Congo, as in Paris.

Through social media platforms like TikTok and YouTube, they are literally spreading the word, reshaping the French language from African countries that were once colonized by France.

A young rapper who goes by the stage name Marla (left), practices her act with other rappers on a rooftop in Abidjan.
Arlette Bashizi for The New York Times

"We've tried to rap in pure French, but nobody was listening to us," said Jean Patrick Niambé, known as Dofy, a 24-year-old Ivorian hip-hop artist listening to Marla on the rooftop. "So we create words from our own realities, and then they spread."

The youth population in Africa is surging while the rest of the world grays. Demographers predict that by 2060, up to 85 percent of French speakers will live on the African continent. In the 1960s, 90 percent of French speakers lived in Western countries.

"French flourishes every day in Africa," said Souleymane Bachir Diagne, a Senegalese professor of French at Columbia University. "This creolized French finds its way in the books we read, the sketches we watch on television, the songs we listen to."

Nearly half of the countries in Africa were at one time French colonies or protectorates, and most of them use French as their official language.

But France has faced growing resentment in recent years in many of these countries for both its colonial legacy and continuing influence. Some countries have evicted French ambassadors and troops, while others target the French language itself. Some West African novelists write in local languages as an act of artistic resistance. The ruling junta in Mali has stripped French of its official status, and a similar move is underway in Burkina Faso.

The backlash has not gone unnoticed in France, where the evolution of French provokes debate, if not angst, among some intellectuals. President Emmanuel Macron of France said in a 2019 speech: "France must take pride in being essentially one country among others that learns, speaks, writes in French."

The language laboratory

In the sprawling Adjamé market in Abidjan, there are thousands of small stalls selling electronics, clothes, counterfeit medicine and food. The market is a perfect laboratory in which to study Nouchi, a slang once crafted by petty criminals, but which has taken over the country in under four decades.

Some former members of Abidjan's gangs, who helped invent Nouchi, now work as guards patrolling the market's alleys, where "jassa men" — young hustlers — sell goods. It is here that new expressions are born.

Germain-Arsène Kadi, a professor of literature at the Alassane Ouattara University in Ivory Coast, walked deep into the market one morning carrying with him the Nouchi dictionary he wrote.

At a street restaurant with plastic tables and chairs, the owner gathered a few jassa men to use their favorite words while they drank Vody, a mix of vodka and energy drink.

"They're going to hit you," the owner said in French, which alarmed me until they explained that the French verb for "hit," frapper, had the opposite meaning there: Those jassa men would treat us well — which they did, throwing out dozens of new words and expressions.

Mr. Kadi frantically scribbled down new words on a notepad, saying repeatedly, "One more for the dictionary."

It's nearly impossible to know which word crafted on the streets of Abidjan might spread, travel or even survive.

"Go," meaning "girlfriend" in Ivory Coast, was entered into the well-known French dictionary Le Robert this year.

In Abidjan this year, people began to call a boyfriend "mon pain" — French for "my bread." Improvisations soon proliferated: "pain choco" is a cute boyfriend. A sugary bread, a sweet one. A bread just out of the oven is a hot partner.

The expression has spread on social media, reaching neighboring Burkina Faso and the Democratic Republic of Congo, thousands of miles away. It hasn't reached France yet. But Ivorians like to joke about which expressions French people will pick up, often years, if not decades, later.

Youth on Yoff Beach in Dakar, Senegal, once a French colony. The youth population in Africa is surging, and by 2060, demographers say, 85 percent of French speakers will live on the continent.
Hannah Reyes Morales for The New York Times

写真：The New York Times/Redux/アフロ

"If French becomes more mixed, then visions of the world it carries will change," said Josué Guébo, an Ivorian poet. "And if Africa influences French from a linguistic point of view, it will likely influence it from an ideological one."

Painful past, uncertain future

Le Magnific — the stage name for Jacques Silvère Bah — is one of Ivory Coast's most famous standup comedians, renowned for his plays on words and imitations of West African accents.

But as a young boy learning French in school, he was forbidden to speak Wobé, his own language, he said. His French was initially so poor.

"We had to learn fast, and in a painful way," said the 45-year-old Mr. Silvère one afternoon, before he took the stage at a standup comedy festival in Abidjan.

Across French-speaking West and Central African countries, French is seldom used at home and is rarely the first language, instead restricted to school, work, business or administration.

According to a 2022 survey released by the French Organization of the Francophonie, the primary organization for promoting French language and culture, 77 percent of respondents in Africa described French as the "language of the colonizer." About 57 percent said it was an imposed language.

Sometimes the methods of imposing it were brutal, scholars say. At school in many French colonies, children speaking in their mother tongue were beaten or forced to wear an object around their necks known as a "symbol" — often a smelly object or an animal bone.

Still, many African countries adopted French as their official language when they gained independence, in part to cement their national identities.

At the festival, Le Magnific and other standup comedians threw jibes in French, drawing laughter from the audience.

"What makes our humor Pan-African is the French language," said the festival's organizer, Mohamed Mustapha, known across West Africa by his stage name, Mamane. A comedian from Niger, Mamane has a program listened to by millions around the world on Radio France Internationale.

Today, more than a third of Ivorians speak French, according to the International Organization of the Francophonie. In Tunisia and the Democratic Republic of Congo — the world's largest French-speaking country — it is more than half.

But in many Francophone countries, governments struggle to hire enough French-speaking teachers.

"African children are still learning in French in extremely difficult conditions," said Francine Quéméner, a program specialist at the International Organization of the Francophonie. "They must learn to count, write, read in a language they don't fully grasp, with teachers who themselves don't always feel secure speaking French."

Still, Ms. Quéméner said French had long escaped France's control.

"French is an African language and belongs to Africans," she said. "The decentralization of the French language is a reality."

France notices

Hip-hop, now dominating the French music industry, is injecting new words, phrases and concepts from Africa into France's suburbs and cities.

One of the world's most famous French-speaking pop singers is Aya Nakamura, originally from Mali. Many of the most streamed hip-hop artists are of Moroccan, Algerian, Congolese or Ivorian origins.

"Countless artists have democratized French music with African slang," said Elvis Adidiema, a Congolese music executive with Sony Music Entertainment. "The French public, from all backgrounds, has become accustomed to those sounds."

But some in France are slow to embrace change. Members of the French Academy, the 17th-century institution that publishes an official dictionary of the French language, have been working on the same edition for the past 40 years.

On a recent evening Dany Laferrière, a Haitian-Canadian novelist and the only Black member of the academy, walked the gilded corridors of the Academy's building, on the left bank of the Seine River. He and his fellow academicians were reviewing whether to add to the dictionary the word "yeah," which appeared in French in the 1960s.

"French is about to make a big leap, and she's wondering how it's going to go," Mr. Laferrière said of the French language.

He paused, stared at the Seine through the window, and corrected himself. "They, not she. They are now multiple versions of French that speak for themselves. And that is the greatest proof of its vitality."

Notes

1 アビジャンはコートジボワール最大の都市で，アフリカのフランス語圏の国々の中におけるファッション，音楽，メディア，デジタルなど，経済活動の中心地．多くの政治機関と外国大使館が置かれ，全アフリカの都市の中で6番目に人口が多い．

2 フランス学士院は国立の学術機関で，言語，文芸，科学，芸術，政治学の5つのアカデミーで構成されるフランス文化の伝統と歴史の象徴ともいえる場所である．なかでもアカデミー・フランセーズは1635年に創設され，フランス語の純粋性と正当性を維持し，新語や外来語の導入を管理するという目的を持つ最古のアカデミーで，アカデミー辞典と呼ばれるフランス語の辞書の編纂を行なっている．アカデミー辞典は1694年に初版が出版されたのち，8回改編され現在に至っている．最新版は1992年．

3 Nouchi は主にアビジャンで使われるカジュアルなスラング．フランス語の中に現地語や英語起源の語彙が混じったり，標準フランス語とは違う意味でフランス語の語彙が使われたりする．

4 Aya Nakamura は1995年アフリカのマリ生まれ，フランス育ちのアフロポップシンガー．フランスだけでなく世界中で，フランス語で歌うアーティストとして絶大な人気があり，2024年のパリオリンピック開会式でもパフォーマンスを披露した．日本人と血縁関係はなく，Nakamura は芸名で，ミュージックビデオに漢字や片仮名を用いるなど，日本のテイストを取り込んでいる．フランスのファッション雑誌の表紙を飾るなど，ファッションアイコンとしても注目されている．

Post-reading

A: Word Match
Write the appropriate description letter in the empty column next to the compounds.

1. Gilded hallways/ corridors		a.	Still having an effect even after the original cause has stopped or gone.
2. Official Dictionary		b.	Imitation or fake drugs.
3. Booming populations		c.	Rarefied atmosphere; a place so elite it is as if the walls are painted gold.
4. Colonial legacy		d.	The language you grow up with.
5. Artistic resistance		e.	The government or academically accepted source for the definition of words in a language.
6. Continuing influence		f.	Wrote as quickly as possible.
7. Counterfeit medicine		g.	Fighting against something through the use of writing, painting, performance etc.
8. Petty criminals		h.	Get used to.
9. Frantically scribbled		i.	Rapidly growing number of people.
10. Standup comedians		j.	Completely understood.
11. Mother tongue		k.	Entertainers who make people laugh by telling their stories and jokes alone on a stage.
12. Gained independence		l.	The emotional, psychological, historical structure and linguistic leftovers of imperialism.
13. Fully grasped		m.	Got freedom from the control of another person or country.
14. Become accustomed		n.	Small time thieves.

B: Comprehension Questions
1. Where is French changing?
2. What is spurring on the infusion of African words into the French language?
3. Which African countries are literally spreading the word through social media?
4. Where do demographers predict that 85% of French speakers will live by 2060?
5. Why is there growing resentment against France in recent years?
6. What have African countries done about this resentment?
7. Who is worried by this linguistic backlash?
8. Where are new African Nouchi/French expressions being born?
9. What did the owner of the café, where Mr. Kadi interviewed the jassa men, mean when he said "They're going to hit you?"
10. What do the terms "mon pain," (my bread) and "pain choco,"(chocolate croissant) mean?
11. According to Josué Guébo, how else will Africa influence France besides linguistically?
12. Where is French most used in Africa?

13. What percentage of respondents in Africa referred to French as the language of the colonizer?
14. Despite the French forcing their language often violently on Africans, why have so many countries adopted it?

C: Discussion Questions
1. Were you aware that French was so widely spoken in Africa?
2. Are you worried that the influx of English words into your language is altering it for the worse?
3. Do you think the government should control the use of words in your language to preserve it?
4. Is there such a thing as a pure language or are all languages mixed and continually evolving?
5. Do you think we need a world language?
6. What are some words of other languages that you have adopted thanks to music, movies, etc.?

D: Research Activities
1. What are the top 10 most spoken languages in the world?
2. How many different dialects of English are there in England?
3. How many distinct dialects are there in Japan?
4. What is the population of Africa? French speaking Africa? English speaking Africa?
5. What are the birth rates in Africa compared to your country?
6. Which continent is predicted to be the most populous in the next 50 years?

Unit 3
Gender Neutral? A Debate Over Spanish Words

Pre-reading

A: Crossword
Match the words in the Word Bank to their descriptions to fill in the crossword.

Word Bank

Activist	Adopted	Alien	Backlash	Banned	Categorized
Degrade	Gendered	Genitalia	Ideological	Inclusive	Linguist
Modified	Morphology	Neutral	Nonbinary	Ostracized	Prohibition
Scandalized	Sexist	Stymied	Trans		

Across
1. (v.) Past participle. Use, choose to follow, take up and practice as one's own.
3. (n.) Private parts. Sex organs. Crotch.
6. (v.) Past participle. Arranged into groups based on certain set ideas.
8. (n.) A strong adverse reaction to a recent political or social issue.
11. (v.) Simple past. To prohibit by legal means. Disallow or stop the use of.
12. (n.) Prejudice or discrimination against people based on their gender, especially language or behavior towards women.
17. (n.) A law or rule forbidding something.
18. (adj.) Adhering to a certain theory, dogma or set of ideas.
19. (v.) Past participle. Offending traditional moral or social sense.
20. (adj.) Not aligned with a political, ideological or sexual grouping.
21. (adj.) Not restricted to two things. A person who identifies with a gender that is neither entirely male or female.

Down
1. (n.) People who vigorously take up a cause to reform society.
2. (v.) To put someone down. To demote.
4. (n.) A person who studies or is conversant in several languages.
5. (adj.) Belonging to another group, place, nation or thing.
7. (adj.) Short for transgender: a person whose identifies with the opposite sex.
9. (v.) Simple past. To block or obstruct.
10. (adj.) Open to and permissive of all, especially the historically excluded.
13. (v.) Past participle. To be exiled from a group, avoided and rejected.
14. (v) Past participle. Identified or treated as either male or female.
15. (n.) A study and description of word formation in language.
16. (v.) Past participle. To make minor or fundamental changes, to make less extreme. To limit the meaning grammatically.

B: Discussion Questions
1. What do you know about and think about gender neutral language?
2. Have you ever been corrected by someone about your use of their pronoun? (e.g. Referred to someone as "he", then be told their pronoun is "she")
3. Are you bothered by the jobs, roles and activities your society expects you to do as a male or as a female? Do you feel there are social limitations concerning gender?
4. Do you think we should change our language to not offend or exclude various groups of people?
5. Is there discrimination against transgender people in your country?

C: Reading Graphs, Maps and Statistics
Based on the map and infographic on the next page:
1. Which country has introduced a new gender neutral pronoun?
2. Which kind of culture (developed high technological, agricultural or indigenous) are most inclusive?
3. Name 4 no gender languages.
4. The Romance languages and Arabic have _____ & _____ genders.
5. What peoples and/or countries have animate and inanimate pronouns?

Map of Gender in Language

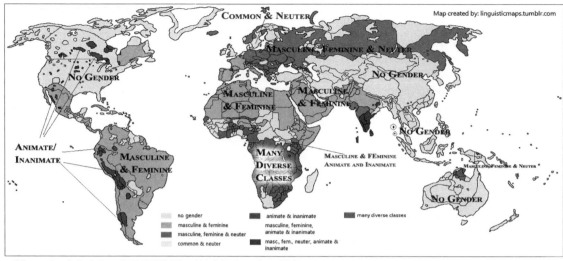

reddit.com/media?url=https%3A%2F%2Fi.redd.it%2Fukpqy5y9w8361.png

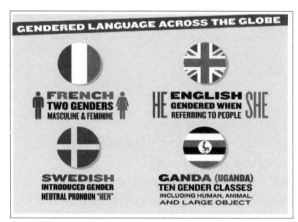

https://gsws390spring18jlputz.sites.wm.edu/2018/04/19/gendering-in-language-and-the-weight-of-words/

By Ana Lankes July 20, 2022

1	amigos, todos, bienvenidos → Note 1
9	masculine or feminine 「（文法上の）男性・女性」
10	gender-neutral language 「男性・女性を区別しない言葉遣い」
13	inclusive 「包括的な」
14	academics 「学者，教育関係者」

BUENOS AIRES — Instead of "amigos," the Spanish word for "friends," some Spanish speakers use "amigues." In place of "todos," or "all," some write "todxs." And some signs that would say "bienvenidos," or "welcome," now say bienvenid@s.

The changes, which had been informally adopted by teachers in schools across Buenos Aires, were an effort to include people who don't identify as male or female in a language where many words are categorized as either masculine or feminine.

Similar gender-neutral language is being increasingly introduced across the rest of Latin America, as well as in other languages, including English and French, by supporters who say it helps create a more inclusive society.

But to some Spanish speakers, including many academics and politicians, the changes degrade a language spoken by a half-billion people around the world.

In June, the city government in Buenos Aires, the nation's capital, banned teachers from using any gender-neutral words during class and in communications with parents. The city's education minister said such language violated the rules of Spanish and stymied students' reading comprehension.

The policy, among the first anywhere to forbid the use of gender-neutral language, provoked a swift backlash. Argentina's top education official criticized the rule and at least five organizations, a mix of gay rights and civil rights groups, have filed lawsuits seeking to overturn it.

Jaime Perczyk, Argentina's education minister, compared the measure to prohibitions against left-handed writing under the fascist dictatorship of Francisco Franco in Spain. "They thought they were correcting something, but it goes much deeper," he said, explaining that students use gender-neutral language as a tool to fight sexist attitudes in Argentine culture.

In Romance languages, including Spanish, French, Italian and Portuguese, the debate over gender-neutral terminology can be particularly fierce because all grammar is gendered.

Gender-neutral language has scandalized linguistic purists. The Royal Academy in Spain, considered by many as the gatekeeper of the Spanish language, described the use of "e," "@," and "X" — which are used in place of the "o" and "a" that often signify a word's gender — as "alien to the morphology of Spanish" in a 2020 report.

Last year, France's education minister recommended avoiding inclusive writing in schools. A prominent French dictionary triggered outrage last October after it added, "iel," a gender-neutral singular pronoun.

The debate has also become part of an emerging culture war in Latin America. In December, Uruguay's public education agency issued a memo limiting the use of inclusive language to be "in accordance with the rules of the Spanish language."

Proposals to ban gender-neutral language in schools or government documents have been pushed in Peru, some states in Mexico, and in at least 34 municipalities and states in Brazil.

Gender-neutral language has also become an issue in October's election in Brazil. The country's president, Jair Bolsonaro, who is seeking a second term, told reporters in December during a discussion about education that "the gays' gender-neutral language" is "screwing up our kids."

The debate is also playing out in the United States, where the gender-neutral term "Latinx" was added to a widely used dictionary in 2018. But even among Hispanic people, many have not heard of the term and few — mainly young college-educated women — use it, according to a survey in 2019 by the Pew Research Center.

The push for changes to Romance languages originated among feminists in at least the 1970s who challenged the use of the generic masculine, a grammatical rule in which the masculine form takes precedence when referring to a group of people if the group includes even one man. (In Spanish, five girls are "las niñas," but once a boy joins, they become "los niños.")

In France, instead of using "chers étudiants," the masculine form of "dear students," feminists promoted the use of double forms that included a feminine spelling, such as "chers étudiants et chères étudiantes," said Heather Burnett, a linguist at France's national research agency.

Today, a new wave of activists is going further. Many transgender people want to erase grammatical gender terms altogether. Instead of using "queridos alumnos y queridas alumnas" ("dear students" in male and female form), they prefer, for example, to use "querides alumnes."

The movement around language, some experts say, is part of a broader challenge to the way society perceives gender.

"What they are questioning on a deeper, ideological level is that gender is not connected to your genitalia and that it does not only come in pairs," said Rodrigo Borba, a professor of applied linguistics at the Federal University of Rio de Janeiro.

Argentina is a surprising place for such a debate because it has largely embraced transgender rights. In 2012, it became one of the first countries in the world to allow people to change their gender on official documents without requiring the intervention of a doctor or a therapist.

Last year, it adopted a measure requiring that 1 percent of all public sector jobs be set aside for transgender people. Those who identify as nonbinary are allowed to mark an "X" on official documents, rather than check off male or female.

In Buenos Aires, the city's education minister, Soledad Acuña, said the new rule on inclusive language is not intended to be a ban. The ministry published several guides on how to be inclusive using traditional Spanish grammar. They suggest, for example, writing "los/as estudiantes" or using neutral words like "personas" or "people."

But some students said the new language decree left them feeling ostracized.

"They put us all in the same box — you are either female or male," said Agostina Fernández Tirra, 17, who identifies as nonbinary and attends a public school in Buenos Aires. "Those of us in the middle, who are neither male nor female, it's like they don't even consider you."

Some parents and teachers have cheered the rule. Gender-neutral language "is not even that inclusive," said Vanina María Casali, the principal of a primary school in Palermo, an upscale Buenos Aires neighborhood. "In our school, there are kids with learning difficulties, and such language makes it even harder for them to learn."

What influence, if any, gender-neutral language has on reading comprehension is unclear, said Florencia Salvarezza, a neuroscientist in Argentina, because little research has been done on the subject.

But, she added, "there is no way to create a syllable in Spanish with the 'x' or the '@' because they are not vowels," she said. "That might confuse young children."

Still, some believe that despite the rule the use of gender-neutral language will continue to expand.

"Language is something that's always being modified," says Alexandra Rodríguez, an after-school volunteer at a community center. "It's alive because we are alive — and it will keep on changing."

16 learning difficulties 「学習困難」
20 reading comprehension 「読解力」

Notes

1 スペイン語の amigos, todos, bienvenidos はいずれも男性複数形.（女性複数形の場合は amigas, todas, bienvenidas となる.）
2 フランシスコ・フランコ (1982-1975) はスペインの軍人で政治家. スペイン内戦で反乱軍を率いて頭角を現した. 1936 年に新政府を樹立して国家元首に就任した後は独裁的権力を掌握し, 1975 年の死去まで影響力を持ち続けた.
3 ロマンス語とは, インド・ヨーロッパ語族のうちラテン語から分化, 派生した諸言語をさす. スペイン語, ポルトガル語, イタリア語, フランス語, ルーマニア語など.
4 ノンバイナリーとは, 自分を男性・女性のどちらかの性別だとは考えない性自認のこと.

Post-reading

A: Word Match

Write the appropriate description letter in the empty column next to the compounds.

1. Informally adopted		a.	Something that is more important and comes before another issue, custom, or thing.
2. Gender-neutral		b.	A country run by a right wing authoritarian ruler.
3. Inclusive society		c.	A legal proclamation concerning speaking and writing.
4. Fascist dictatorship		d.	The use of words which are acceptable and welcoming to all people.
5. Sexist attitudes		e.	Unofficially used and followed.
6. Linguistic purists		f.	He, him, his. Boys, men, guys.
7. Romance languages		g.	Values that are prejudiced against the opposite gender.
8. Takes precedence		h.	Scholars of language or others who think language should follow strict unchanging rules.
9. Generic masculine		i.	Not identifying as any particular sex. Neither male nor female.
10. Language decree		j.	Italian, French, Portuguese, Spanish, Romanian.
11. Transgender rights		k.	A civilization that accepts and recognizes all kinds of people and gender orientation.
12. Inclusive language		l.	Ethical and/or legal social protection for people who identify as the opposite gender of their birth sex.

B: Comprehension Questions

1. Why are teachers in Buenos Aires, Argentina adopting new forms of traditional words such as "amigues" instead of "amigos", their old word for friends?
2. What kind of society are supporters of gender-neutral language trying to create?
3. According to the Education Minister, why did the city government ban teachers from using gender-neutral words during classes?
4. Who and which groups were provoked to a swift backlash by this ban?
5. To what did the country's education minister, Jaime Perczyk, compare the ban?
6. Why does gender-neutral terminology provoke such fierce reactions in Romance languages?
7. Who is considered to be the "gatekeeper" of the Spanish language?
8. Where else in the Americas have proposals been put forth to ban gender-neutral language?
9. What grammatical rule in Romance languages did feminists in the 1970s challenge?
10. Why is Argentina a surprising place for this debate?
11. Why do nonbinary students feel ostracized?
12. Why do some believe that the use of gender-neutral language will continue to expand?

C: Discussion Questions
1. Does your language have gendered language or is it gender-neutral? (think of pronouns, titles etc.)
2. Is this debate happening in your country now?
3. Do you think creating new words to include various gender and sexual orientations is a good idea?
4. Does language have an effect on inclusivity? Is your country an inclusive or exclusive society?
5. Should teachers have the right to introduce new pronouns and words in schools?
6. Should the government have the right to ban certain words in schools?

D: Research Activities
1. Look up and list the various new pronouns in English being suggested by the LGBTQ community.
2. Make a list of words in your native language that are particularly used by men and by women.
3. Are there any laws or trends in your country concerning the use of language in schools?
4. In how many countries is it illegal to be homosexual?
5. What are some of the penalties for homosexuality in these countries?
6. Look up and draw 4 or 5 of the numerous new symbols for various gender identities.

III

Nature and Humanity: a Complex Relationship

Unit 4
Extreme Heat Will Change Us

Pre-reading

A: Crossword

Match the words in the Word Bank to their descriptions to fill in the crossword.

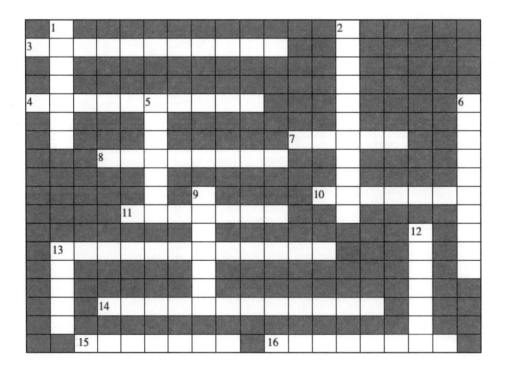

Word Bank

Arduous	Asphalt	Catastrophic	Crimp	Debilitating	Dehydration
Exposure	Extreme	Grueling	Inequality	Inexorable	Intense
Monitor	Scald	Swelter	Thermal	Unrelenting	

Across
3. (adj.) Never ending, persistent. Non stopping, grim, inexorable, stern.
4. (n.) Not of equal status. Subject to unfair laws and rules.
7. (v.) Very hot. Burning, blister, boiling point.
8. (adj.) Hard, arduous, backbreaking, laborious, toilsome. Effort to point exhaustion.
10. (n.) A device that takes signals and displays them on a screen.
11. (n.) Mixed gravel & sand used for paving roads.
13. (adj.) Ruinous, extremely harmful.
14. (adj.) Impairing the strength or vitality.
15. (n.) The furthest, highest, or greatest degree of something.
16. (n.) The act of being subjected to the elements, rain, wind, heat, or some other influencing experience. Vulnerability to the elements.

Down
1. (adj.) Acute, sharp, a feature increased to a heightened degree.
2. (n.) Dryness, desiccation, lack of water.
5. (adj.) Hard, grueling, backbreaking, toilsome. Effort to point exhaustion.
6. (adj.) Never ending, persistent, grim, unrelenting, stern.
9. (adj.) Relating to heat. Designed to retain heat.
12. (v.) To be excessively hot and humid, to sweat and feel faintness.
13. (v.) Pinch, make ridges, kink.

B: Discussion Questions
1. What is the highest temperature you have ever experienced?
2. What is the lowest temperature?
3. Have you ever had to stay in a room without air conditioning on a really hot day? (e.g. 38 degrees Celsius)
4. Have you noticed it getting warmer in your country since you were a child?
5. Have you ever experienced any extreme weather? (typhoons etc.)
6. Have you ever had heat stroke?

C: Reading Graphs, Maps and Statistics
Look at the graphs below and on the next page.

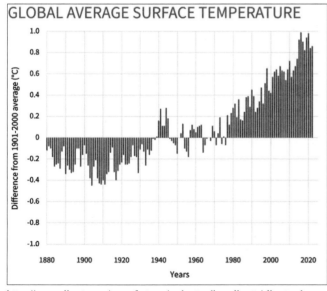

https://www.climate.gov/news-features/understanding-climate/climate-change-global-temperature

1. How much has the global average surface temperature increased since 1880?

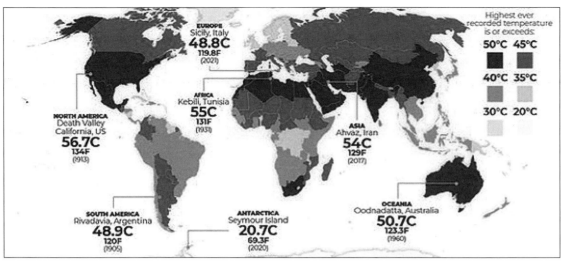

https://www.aljazeera.com/news/2022/7/18/what-is-the-highest-temperature-ever-recorded-in-your-country

2. What is and where is the highest recorded temperature?
3. Mark Iraq on the map.

By Alissa J. Rubin, Ben Hubbard, Josh Holder, Noah Throop,
Emily Rhyne, Jeremy White and James Glanz   Nov. 18, 2022

Health: how heat damages the body

On a treeless street under a blazing sun, Abbas Abdul Karim, a welder with 25 years experience, labors over a metal bench.

Everyone who lives in Basra, Iraq's third-largest city, reckons with intense heat, but for Abbas it is unrelenting. He must do his work during daylight hours to see the iron he deftly bends into swirls for stair railings or welds into door frames.

The heat is so grueling that he never gets used to it. "I feel it burning into my eyes," he says.

Working outside in southern Iraq's scalding summer temperatures isn't just arduous. It can cause long-term damage to the body.

We know the risk for Abbas, because we measured it.

By late morning, the air around Abbas reached a heat index of 52°C, a measure of heat and humidity. That created a high risk for heat stroke — especially with his heavy clothing and the direct sun.

Thermal images show additional heat coming off his equipment, making his workspace even more dangerous.

The body's struggle to sweat and cool itself can cause dehydration and put extra pressure on the kidneys. Over time, this increases the risk of kidney stones and kidney disease.

The heart works harder, too, laboring to pump more blood to the skin and carry heat out of the body.

As Abbas worked, our monitor found that his pulse rose, indicating to experts that his body temperature had risen by about three degrees, which puts dangerously high stress on the heart.

The blood reaching Abbas's brain was probably reduced for about an hour, as the blood flow was needed elsewhere. He felt unsteady and had to stop. "It feels like the heat is coming out of my head," he said.

What Abbas was experiencing wasn't a heatwave. It was just an average August day in Basra, a city on the leading edge of climate change — and a glimpse of the future for much of the planet as human carbon emissions warp the climate.

By 2050, nearly half the world may live in areas that have dangerous levels of heat for at least a month, including Miami, Lagos and Shanghai, according to projections by researchers at Harvard University and the University of Washington.

Just how bad it gets will depend on how much humanity curbs climate change. But some of the far-reaching effects of extreme heat are already inevitable, and they will levy a huge tax on entire societies — their economies, health and way of life.

As we tracked the daily activities of people in Basra and Kuwait City, we documented their heat exposure and how it had transformed their lives.

We saw the tremendous gap between those who have the means to protect themselves and those who do not. We also saw a still more unsettling reality: No one can escape debilitating heat entirely.

Adaptation: how heat destroys our daily life

The heat roused Kadhim Fadhil Enad from sleep. His family's air-conditioner had stopped, and he found himself sweating in the dark.

High temperatures would govern the rest of his day. For him and many others in his city, the growing heat has turned workdays and sleep schedules upside down.

When Kadhim, 25, and his brother, Rahda, left for work just after 4 a.m., it felt like 45 degrees outside.

Kadhim and Radha work in construction as day laborers. In the sweltering summers of southern Iraq, that means racing to finish as much as possible before the sun comes up and ushers in the harshest heat of the day.

Once the sun rose, bleaching the sky and baking the bricks

around them, they barely spoke, conserving their energy for the work at hand.

By 7:22 a.m., it was too hot to keep going on the roof, so they ate breakfast in the shade and switched to indoor tasks. At 9 a.m., they quit for the day.

Even if they can adapt their schedule, as Kadhim has, and start their job in the middle of the night, it is still so hot that exhaustion truncates the workday, reducing productivity and chipping away at earnings.

Extreme heat is altering life across the globe, including in Pakistan, India, Tunisia, Mexico, central China and elsewhere. And the more temperatures rise, the greater the number of workers who will be affected.

Already, the effects of extreme heat add up to hundreds of billions of dollars in lost work each year worldwide.

Inequality: money can't save you

It was 5:30 a.m. in Kuwait city when Abdullah Husain, 36, left his apartment to walk his dogs. The sun had barely risen, but the day was already so sweltering.

In the summer, he said, he has to get the dogs out early, before the asphalt gets so hot that it will burn their paws. "Everything after sunrise is hell," he said.

Abdullah, an assistant professor of environmental sciences at Kuwait University, lives a very different life from Kadhim in Basra. But both men's days are shaped by inexorable heat.

Basra and Kuwait City lie only 130 kilometers apart and usually have the same weather, with summertime temperatures climbing to around 40 degrees for weeks on end.

But in other ways, they are worlds apart. Both places produce oil, but in Kuwait it has produced great wealth and provided citizens with a high standard of living.

This vast economic gap is never clearer than when it comes to how well people can protect themselves from the heat, a divide between rich and poor that is increasingly playing out across the globe.

Abdullah drives to work on broad highways in an air-conditioned car. Kadhim walks to work on streets lined with swiftly rotting garbage.

Abdullah teaches at a heavily air-conditioned university. Even working at night, Kadhim cannot escape his heating world.

Kuwait's tremendous oil wealth allows it to protect people from the heat — but those protections carry their own cost, crimping culture and lifestyle alike.

When the heat hits, people desert parks and outdoor dining areas. Slides, swings and other playground equipment get so hot that they can burn children's legs. Most Kuwaitis avoid going outside at all.

So life has moved indoors. Many Kuwaitis never step outside for longer than it takes to walk to their cars. The rest of life is air-conditioned: where they sleep, exercise, work and socialize.

That affects their health. Despite the abundance of sun, many Kuwaitis suffer from deficiencies of vitamin D, which the body uses sunlight to produce. Many are also overweight.

By the end of the century, Basra, Kuwait City and many other cities will most likely have many more dangerously hot days per year. Just how many depends on what humans do in the meantime.

According to forecasts by researchers at Harvard University, even if humans significantly reduce carbon emissions, by the year 2100, Kuwait City and Basra will experience months of heat and humidity that feel hotter than 40 degrees, far more than they have had in the last decade.

Estimates long into the future are inexact, but scientists agree that the situation will worsen — and could be catastrophic if emissions aren't reined in. In that scenario, Miami, for instance, could experience dangerous heat for nearly half the year.

Abdullah, the professor, said most Kuwaitis don't think about the relationship between burning fossil fuels and the heat.

"People complain about it, but it is not something that registers action or a change of behavior," he said. "They use it to tan or go to the beach, but if it is too hot, they stay home in the air-conditioning."

And since atmospheric emissions don't respect borders, Kuwait City and Basra will continue to get hotter regardless of what they do, unless major emitters like the United States and China change course.

The future: can this place still be a home?

Before Abbas, the welder, was born in 1983, Basra was a greener, cooler city. Groves of date palms softened the temperature, and canals that irrigated Basra's gardens earned it the nickname "the

Venice of the East."

Many of those stately palm groves were being cut down when Abbas was a child, so fewer remained when Kadhim, the construction worker, was growing up in the early 2000s. But even then, the city was still dotted with tamarisks, hearty shrubs that erupted yearly with pink and white flowers.

Now, most of those are gone too. Basra has become a drab city of concrete and asphalt, which soaks up the sun and radiates heat long after sundown.

In the future, many people around the world will migrate to escape the heat. But there will most likely be many others who, like Abbas and Kadhim, lack the resources to make it to a greener country. And richer countries that have already tightened their borders will probably make immigration even more difficult as climate pressures increase.

Abbas and Kadhim both dream of living elsewhere. Abbas wants somewhere "greener," Kadhim somewhere "cooler." Kadhim hopes to marry and have children, and raise them somewhere that has "space for nature."

"The houses will be made of wood, and there will be a forest," he said.

Notes
1 熱指数とは，温度と湿度を用いて気温が実際にはどれくらい暑く感じられるかを算出する体感温度のこと．
12 resource 「資産，予備のお金」

Post-reading

A: Word Match
Write the appropriate description letter in the empty column next to the compounds.

1.	Heat index		a. Temperature, wind and rainfall changes in the earth's weather, especially due to greenhouse gases.
2.	Heat stroke		b. Involving a lot of danger and risk of injury even death.
3.	High risk		c. A very large difference between people or states.
4.	Thermal images		d. A difference between the finances of people or states.
5.	Climate change		e. Subject to high temperatures, usually outside.
6.	Carbon emissions		f. A measure of both temperature and the effects of humidity combined.
7.	Tremendous gap		g. The releasing of gases in the upper regions of the earth's sky.
8.	Heat exposure		h. Pictures of something produced by mapping the heat that comes from it.
9.	Unsettling reality		i. The release into the atmosphere of CO_2
10.	Environmental sciences		j. An illness caused by being in too high temperatures for too long.
11.	Economic gap		k. A disturbing actual situation.
12.	Atmospheric emissions		l. The branch of study involved with changes, especially man made changes, in the natural world.

B: Comprehension Questions
1. What is Abbas doing and where?
2. Why is Abbas in danger of heat stroke? (Include the temperature in your answer).
3. What kinds of health risks can be caused by heat stroke?
4. How much of the world will suffer dangerous levels of heat by 2050?
5. Between who is the tremendous gap in heat exposure?
6. What do most Kuwaitis suffer from due to their moving indoors?
7. How much does the effects of heat cost in lost work each year?
8. Why can't children play on playground equipment in Kuwait?
9. By what year will Basra and Kuwait city experience months of over 40 degrees?
10. What was Basra's nickname and why?
11. How does the lack of trees and the concrete add to the heat?
12. What will many people around the world do to escape the heat in the future?

C: Discussion Questions
1. Do you think you could live in the Middle East?
2. Have you ever noticed the difference between the heat in the city and in the countryside during the summer? Which place was more comfortable?
3. Knowing that concrete makes the places hotter, what is a simple solution for

reducing heat in the cities and suburbs?
4. What can you do to reduce global warming?
5. What are some things individuals can do to not waste electricity?
6. Could you live without air-conditioning?

D: Research Activities
1. Which area of the world is experiencing the greatest rise in temperatures? How many degrees?
2. What were the average August temperatures in your country this year? In the year 2010? 1990? 1970? 1950? 1930? 1910?
3. When did it last snow in Osaka?
4. How often did it snow in Osaka 50 years ago?
5. List ways we can reduce heat in cities and suburbs.
6. What temperature is optimum to set the air-conditioner at to save electricity in the summer?
7. What is the percentage of people in Japan without air-conditioning?
8. Are there any initiatives to plant trees or make green rooftops in Japan?

Unit 5
Pandemic Lockdown Healed and Hurt Nature

Pre-reading

A: Crossword

Match the words in the Word Bank to their descriptions to fill in the crossword.

Word Bank

Abundant	Anthropause	Biomass	Breed	Conservation	Cull
Custodian	Designate	Diversity	Document	Ecologist	Ecosystem
Habitat	Lockdown	Pandemic	Protect	Refuge	Shoreline
Species	Spike				

—46—

Across
2. (adj.) Plentiful, existing in large quantities.
5. (n.) All the plants and living creatures in a particular area related to that specific physical environment.
6. (v.) To have sex and produce children.
7. (n.) A group of animals, plants etc. that are able to reproduce.
8. (n.) A person who studies the environment.
9. (n.) The place where a particular type of animal or plant is normally found.
10. (v.) To record in detail.
12. (n.) A person who takes responsibility for taking care or protecting someone or something.
13. (v.) To kill a number of wild animals from a group to stop it becoming too large.
14. (n.) The total quantity in weight of the plants and animals in a particular area.
15. (v.) To make sure something is not harmed, killed or injured.
16. (n.) The edge of the sea, ocean or lake.
17. (n.) A break in human activity.
18. (n.) A place to shelter or receive protection from danger.

Down
1. (n.) A disease that spreads around the world.
3. (n.) The protection of the natural environment.
4. (v.) To assign a particular name, character or job to someone or something.
7. (n.) A sudden large increase in something.
10. (n.) A range of different people, animals, plants of things.
11. (n.) An official order to control the movement of people because of a dangerous situation.(e.g. a pandemic)

B: Discussion Questions
1. How and where did you spend Covid-19?
2. What were good points about Covid-19? What were bad points?
3. Did you spend more time or less time in nature?
4. Did you notice any changes in the area around where you live, e.g. about the noise, traffic, animal life or pollution?
5. How about your own behavior and character? Was it changed by Covid-19?

C: Reading Graphs, Maps and Statistics
Look at the images below and on the next page.

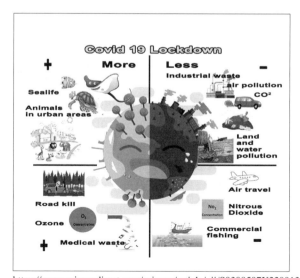

1. What things increased and what things decreased during the pandemic?
2. Can you find other examples of an increase in the number of animals or decrease in pollution?

https://www.sciencedirect.com/science/article/pii/S0308597X2200135X をもとに編注者が作成

3. Why do you think this bear is in the streets?
4. Can you find other similar images?
5. Why were animals found in towns and cities during Covid-19? Why not always?

https://www.mapleridgenews.com/community/jaywalking-bear-in-pitt-meadow-draws-concern-2660326

By Emily Anthes   July 16, 2022

5	out of the picture	「いなくなる」
6	white-tailed eagle	「オジロワシ」
8	protected population	「保護個体群」
9	common murre	「ウミガラス」
	flush	「追い出す」
13	performance	「実績」
19	a body of	「大量の」
	literature	「文献」
21	anthropause → Note 1	
22	resource	「方策」
27	routine	「日常の行動」

In a typical spring, breeding seabirds — and human seabird-watchers — flock to Stora Karlsö, an island off the coast of Sweden.

But in 2020, the Covid-19 pandemic reduced human presence on the island by more than 90 percent. With people out of the picture, white-tailed eagles moved in, becoming much more abundant than usual.

The eagles repeatedly soared past the cliffs where a protected population of common murres laid its eggs, flushing the smaller birds from their ledges.

In the commotion, some eggs tumbled from the cliffs; others were snatched by predators while the murres were away. The murres' breeding performance dropped 26 percent, researchers found.

The pandemic was, and remains, a global human tragedy. But for ecologists, it has also been an opportunity to learn more about how people affect the natural world by documenting what happened when we abruptly stepped back from it.

A growing body of literature paints a complex portrait of the slowdown of human activity that has become known as the "anthropause." Some species clearly benefited from our absence. But other species struggled without human protection or resources.

"Human beings are playing this dual role," said Amanda Bates, an ocean conservation scientist at the University of Victoria in Canada. We are, she said, acting as "threats to wildlife but also being custodians for our environment."

When the pandemic hit, many human routines came to a sudden halt. On April 5, 2020 — the peak of the pandemic lockdowns — 4.4 billion people, or 57 percent of the planet, were under some sort of movement restriction. Driving decreased by more than 40 percent, while air traffic declined by 75 percent.

"We know that humans impact ecosystems by changing the climate, we know that they have dramatic impacts by changing land use, like razing down habitat and building shopping malls," said Christopher Wilmers, a wildlife ecologist at the University of California, Santa Cruz. "But what are the impacts of human mobility itself?"

With humans holed up in their homes — cars stuck in garages, airplanes in hangars, ships in docks — air and water quality improved in some places, scientists found. Noise pollution abated on land and under the sea. Human-disturbed habitats began to recover.

In March 2020, Hawaii's Hanauma Bay Nature Preserve, a popular snorkeling destination, closed and remained shuttered for nearly nine months. "The pandemic reset the visitor impacts to zero," said Ku'ulei Rodgers, a coral reef ecologist at the Hawai'i Institute of Marine Biology.

Without swimmers, water clarity improved by 56 percent, Dr. Rodgers found. Fish density, biomass and diversity increased in waters that had previously been thick with snorkelers.

"All animals are, you know, trying not to die," said Kaitlyn Gaynor, an ecologist at the University of British Columbia. That drive to survive prompts them to keep their distance from potential predators, including humans. "We are noisy and novel and resemble their predators — and in many cases are their predators," Dr. Gaynor said.

The mountain lions that live in the Santa Cruz Mountains of California typically stay away from cities. But after local shelter-in-place orders took effect in 2020, the animals became more likely to select habitats near the urban edge.

Dr. Wilmers speculated that the mountain lions were responding to changes in the urban soundscape, which might typically be filled with human chatter and the rumble of passing cars.

Just north, in a newly hushed San Francisco, white-crowned sparrows began singing more quietly, yet the distance across which they could communicate "more than doubled," researchers found. The birds also began singing at lower frequencies, a shift that is associated with better performance.

But the effects of human absence were nuanced, varying by

species, location and time.

Multiple studies found that as traffic eased in the spring of 2020, the number of wild animals that were struck and killed by cars declined. But the number soon crept back up, even as traffic remained below normal levels, one team of researchers reported.

"Per mile driven, there were more accidents happening during the pandemic," said Joel Abraham, a graduate student at Princeton University. "Animals started using roads. And it was difficult for them to stop, even when traffic started to rebound."

The lockdowns disrupted efforts to control some invasive species. For instance, the pandemic delayed a long-planned project to cull giant, predatory mice from Gough Island, a critical habitat for threatened sea birds in the South Atlantic Ocean. The mice, which likely arrived with 19th-century sailors, attack and feed on bird chicks, often leaving large open wounds. Many chicks succumb to their injuries.

Scientists were set to begin an ambitious mouse-eradication effort when the pandemic hit, delaying the project for a year. In the intervening breeding season, with the vampire mice still running rampant, not one MacGillivray's prion chick — an endangered bird that breeds almost exclusively on Gough — survived.

It is another illustration of humanity's dual roles: The mice are only on Gough because humans took them there. "But now we absolutely need humans to cull them," Dr. Bates said.

These kinds of impacts added up all over the world, she said, as local conservation, education and monitoring programs were disrupted or deprived of funding. Spikes in wildlife poaching and persecution, as well as illegal logging and mining, were reported in multiple countries.

Economic insecurity might have driven some of this activity, but experts believe that it was also made possible by lapses in human protection, including reduced staffing in parks and preserves and even an absence of tourists, whose presence might typically discourage illegal activity.

Understanding these mechanisms can help experts design programs and policies that channel our influence more thoughtfully.

"If we strengthen the role as custodians and then continue to regulate pressures, we can really tilt the role of humans in the environment to an overwhelmingly positive role," said Carlos Duarte, a marine ecologist at King Abdullah University of Science and Technology in Saudi Arabia.

Researchers found that in the pandemic summer of 2020, loggerhead sea turtles that nest on the Greek island of Zakynthos spent more time close to shore in the warmer waters that are optimal for egg development than they had in previous years.

The results suggest that tourists are driving sea turtles into cooler waters, slowing egg development and potentially reducing the number of eggs the animals lay during the short nesting season, said Gail Schofield, a conservation ecologist at Queen Mary University of London.

Halting all tourism is not possible, she acknowledged. But designating a stretch of the shoreline as a protected turtle habitat and prohibiting swimming there in the early summer could provide an important refuge for the animals, she said.

Other changes could pay dividends, too: Building wildlife crossings over highways could keep some animals from becoming road kill, while mandating quieter car engines and boat propellers could curb noise pollution on land and at sea.

"No one can say anymore that we can't change the whole world in a year, because we can," Dr. Bates said. "We did."

Notes

1. anthropause とは，anthropo-（人類）と pause（休止）を組み合わせた単語で，2020年に始まったパンデミックの中で登場した新語．コロナ禍で多くの人々の移動や活動が世界的に大幅に減少，停滞した状態をさす．
2. Gough Island は南大西洋にあるイギリス領の孤島．気象観測所のスタッフが常駐している他は定住者はいない．20種類以上の海鳥の繁殖地として重要な島で，ユネスコの世界自然遺産として登録されている．

Post-reading

A: Word Match

Write the appropriate description letter in the empty column next to the compounds.

1. Global tragedy		a. A strong effect on something or someone.
2. Pandemic lockdown		b. Animals or plants brought to a new area where they do not belong and do not have natural predators.
3. Dramatic impact		c. The cutting down of trees without permission.
4. Razing down		d. The illegal hunting of animals in a private or protected area.
5. Human mobility		e. An earth wide catastrophe.
6. Human disturbed		f. A biologist who tries to preserve an environment or habitat.
7. Invasive species		g. Ruined or altered by peoples' actions.
8. Conservation ecologist		h. Spreading all over an area without control.
9. Running rampant		i. A government decree for people to stay at home during a virus outbreak.
10. Wildlife crossings		j. Bridges and protected lanes for animals to use to avoid being hit by cars etc.
11. Wildlife poaching		k. The destroying, or cutting down of something.
12. Illegal logging		l. Movement of people.

B: Comprehension Questions

1. Why did the murres breeding performance drop 26% after human seabird watchers declined by 90% during the Covid-19 pandemic in 2020?
2. Why was the pandemic an opportunity for ecologists?
3. Why has the pandemic been called the "anthropause"?
4. How did species react to the decline of human presence?
5. By what percentages did car and air traffic decline during the pandemic?
6. As cars, airplanes and ships were parked in garages, hangers and docks, what improved and what declined in nature?
7. By how much did Hanauma Bay water clarity improve without swimmers and snorkelers?
8. Why did mountain lions start living closer to the city edge in 2020?
9. Why despite the decline in traffic were there more animals killed per mile driven during the pandemic?
10. What negative human activities spiked during the pandemic and why?
11. Marine biologist, Carlos Duarte believes we can tilt the role of humans to an overwhelmingly positive role if we do what?
12. Since stopping tourism is not possible, what could people do to reduce their impact on wild species, such as sea turtles?

C: Discussion Questions
1. Did you see, hear, or read about any animals being in urban areas during Covid-19?
2. Knowing that a decline in noise from traffic increased animal presence, what can we do in the future to increase animal life in our world?
3. Some countries create corridors for wildlife, such as wide grass bridges over highways. Would you like to see more wildlife around your country? What can you do?
4. Where in Japan is there a mix of nature and city? (e.g. Animals in the streets.)
5. What other ideas can you think of to make our urban areas more natural?
6. Do you think integration of animals and human life is a good idea, or should we provide more space for animals separate from human life?

D: Research Activities
1. Look up the percentages of animals that increased during the Covid-19 lockdown.
2. Look up the percentages of animals that decreased during the Covid-19 lockdown.
3. List a few species whose population benefits from human interaction.
4. List a few species that have gone extinct due to human existence.
5. What species have recovered from near extinction and what actions saved them?
6. Name a few NGOs that work hard to save animals.

IV

Trying to Lessen Our Footprint

Unit 6
South Korea Turns Scraps Into Energy

Pre-reading

A: Crossword
Match the words in the Word Bank to their descriptions to fill in the crossword.

Word Bank

Automated	Biogas	Cling	Debris	Dehydrated	Discharged
Facilities	Fertilizer	Fiber	Grinder	Incinerators	Landfills
Marinated	Methane	Odors	Potent	Process	Purified
Sludgy	Stench	Waste			

Across
1. (adj.) Soaked (usually food) in a liquid or sauce.
2. (n.) A device for crushing things into fine particles.
4. (n.) Bad smell.
6. (n.) Dug out areas of soil into which garbage is dumped.
7. (n.) A substance that makes soil better for growing crops.
8. (n.) Thread like structured foods good for digestion.
12. (v.) Past participle. A thing able to operate on its own.
13. (n.) Factories for burning waste.
14. (n.) Smells.
15. (n.) An action or series of actions towards an end product.
17. (adj.) Muddy, wet, slushy settled mass.
18. (adj.) Powerful, effective.
19. (v.) Past participle. Released, or let out.

Down
1. (n.) A colorless odorless gas (CH_4) that is a product of decomposing organic matter.
3. (v.) Past participle. Lacking in water.
5. (n.) Rejected material. Garbage, rubbish, sewage.
7. (n.) A place or things built for a particular purpose to make an action or operation easier.
9. (n.) A mixture of carbon dioxide and methane caused by the decomposition of organic wastes and used as a fuel.
10. (v.) Past participle. Made clear and free of any pollutants.
11. (n.) The remains of something broken down or destroyed.
16. (v.) To hold onto tightly.

B: Discussion Questions

1. What does your family do with your food scraps or leftovers from meals?
2. Have you ever worked in a restaurant or super market? How much food was thrown away?
3. Where do you think all the garbage produced at homes, restaurants and super markets goes?
4. Do you live near an incinerator? Or have you ever seen images of landfills?
5. Have you even smelt the stench of rotting food?
6. What might we do with all this waste? What is another way to deal with it?

C: Reading Graphs, Maps and Statistics

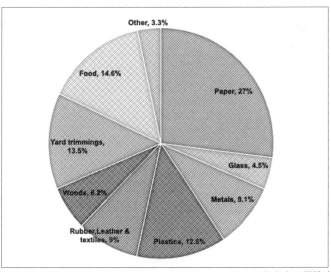

1. What percentage of solid waste does food make up of total waste?
2. Which item to you is most surprising? Why?

https://archive.epa.gov/epawaste/nonhaz/municipal/web/html/ をもとに編注者が作成

https://www.statista.com/statistics/1252704/largest-dump-sites-by-annual-volume-worldwide/

3. Which country generates the most waste?
4. Which region?

https://www.statista.com/statistics/1252704/largest-dump-sites-by-annual-volume-worldwide/

5. What are the criteria for the Yale Environmental Performance Index?
6. What is the difference between the two maps? Why does the U.S. produce the most waste, yet gets a good score on the Yale index?

By John Yoon June 14, 2023

SEOUL — Around the world, most of the 1.4 billion tons of food thrown away each year goes to landfills. As it rots, it pollutes water and soil and releases huge amounts of methane, one of the most potent greenhouse gases.

But in South Korea, which banned food scraps from its landfills almost 20 years ago, the vast majority of the waste gets turned into animal feed, fertilizer and fuel for heating homes.

Food waste is one of the biggest contributors to climate change, not only because of the methane but also because the energy and resources that went into its production and transport have been wasted.

The system in South Korea, which keeps about 90 percent of discarded food out of landfills and incinerators, has been studied by governments around the world. Officials from China, Denmark and elsewhere have toured South Korea's facilities. New York City, which will require all residents to separate their food waste from other trash by next fall, has been observing the Korean system for years.

While a number of cities have comparable programs, few other countries do what South Korea does on a national scale. That is because of the cost, said Paul West, a senior scientist with Project Drawdown, a research group that studies ways to reduce carbon emissions.

Although individuals and businesses pay a small fee to discard food waste, the program costs South Korea about $600 million a year, according to the country's Ministry of Environment.

Despite the cost, experts say it should be emulated. "The South Korea example makes it possible to reduce emissions at a larger scale," he said.

South Korea's culinary tradition tends to result in uneaten food. Small side dishes — sometimes a few, sometimes more than a dozen — accompany most meals. For years, practically all of those leftovers went into the ground.

But the country's mountainous terrain limits how many landfills can be built, and how far from residential areas they can be. In 1995, the government introduced mandatory recycling of paper and plastic, but food scraps continued to be buried along with other trash.

Political support for changing that was driven by people living near landfills, who complained about the smells, said Kee-Young

At the end of the day, the food waste from Mr. Lee's restaurant goes into a special bin. A sticker proves he has paid for the disposal.

写真：The New York Times/Redux/ アフロ

2	stew	「汁もの，スープ」
3	water content	「水分量」

11	Jongno Stew Village	「チョンノ・シチュー・ヴィレッジ」
	Dobong district	「道峰（トボン）区」
12	pollock stew	「干しダラのスープ」
	kimchi jjigae	「キムチチゲ」
14	bean sprouts	「もやし」
15	perilla leaves	「エゴマの葉」
18	err on the side of abundance	「多く取りすぎるという失敗をする」→ Note 1
22	designated bin	「指定のゴミ箱」

Yoo, a researcher at the government-run Seoul Institute who has advised cities on handling food waste. Because stews are a staple of Korean cuisine, discarded food here tends to have a high water content, which means greater volume and worse odors.

"When all of that went to waste, it emitted a terrible stench," Mr. Yoo said.

Since 2005, it's been illegal to send food waste to landfills. Local governments have built hundreds of facilities for processing it. Consumers, restaurant owners, truck drivers and others are part of the network that gets it collected and turned into something useful.

At Jongno Stew Village, a popular lunch spot in the Dobong district of northern Seoul, pollock stew and kimchi jjigae are the best sellers. But no matter the order, Lee Hae-yeon, the owner, serves small side dishes of kimchi, tofu, boiled bean sprouts and marinated perilla leaves.

Customers can help themselves to more, and "people are going to take more than they're going to eat," Mr. Lee said. "Koreans like to err on the side of abundance when it comes to food."

Mr. Lee pays a price for that: about 2,800 won, a little over $2, for every 20 liters of food he throws out. All day, leftovers go into a bucket in the kitchen, and at closing time Mr. Lee empties it into a designated bin outside. On the lid, he attaches a sticker purchased from the district — evidence that he's paid for the disposal.

In the morning, companies hired by the district empty those bins. Park Myung-joo and his team start rolling through the streets at 5 a.m., tearing the stickers off the bins and dumping the contents into their truck's tank.

They work every day except Sundays. "Even waiting a day would cause huge amounts of waste to pile up," Mr. Park said.

Around 11 a.m., they get to Dobong's processing facility, where they unload the sludgy mess.

Debris — bones, seeds, shells — is picked out by hand. (Dobong's plant is one of the last in the nation where this step isn't automated.) A conveyor belt carries the waste into a grinder, which reduces it to small pieces. Anything that isn't easily shredded, like plastic bags, is filtered out and incinerated.

Then the waste is baked and dehydrated. The moisture goes into pipes leading to a water treatment plant, where some of it is used to produce biogas. The rest is purified and discharged into a nearby stream.

What's left of the waste is ground into the final product: a dry, brown powder that smells like dirt. It's a feed supplement for chickens and ducks, rich in protein and fiber, said Sim Yoon-sik, the facility's manager, and given away to any farm that wants it.

Inside the plant, the strong odors cling to fabric and hair. But outside, they are barely noticeable. Pipes run through the building, purifying the air via a chemical process before the exhaust system expels it.

Other plants work differently. At the biogas facility in Goyang, a Seoul suburb, the food waste — nearly 70,000 tons annually — undergoes anaerobic digestion. It sits in large tanks for up to 35 days while bacteria does its work, breaking the organic matter down and creating biogas, consisting mainly of methane and carbon dioxide.

The biogas is sold to a local utility, which says it's used to heat 3,000 homes in Goyang. What solid matter remains is mixed with wood chips to create fertilizer, which is given away.

Every ton of food waste that rots in a landfill emits greenhouse gases equivalent to 800 pounds of carbon dioxide, researchers have found. Turning it into biogas cuts that in half, said Lee Chang-gee, an engineer at the Goyang plant.

Critics note that for all its benefits, South Korea's program hasn't attained one of its goals: getting people to throw away less

Eom Jung-suk scanning her card to open the food waste bin at her Seoul apartment complex.

写真：The New York Times/Redux/ アフロ

2	steady	「横ばいの」

food. The amount of discarded food nationwide has stayed more or less steady over the years, according to data from the Ministry of Environment.

The system has had other flaws. There have been scattered complaints: In Deogyang, a district of Goyang, residents of one village said the odor from a processing facility was once so bad that they couldn't leave their windows open. That plant has been inactive since 2018 because of neighbors' protests.

"When the plant shut down, all the problems disappeared," said a Deogyang resident, Mo Sung Yun, 68.

But most of the plants nationwide have drawn few serious complaints from neighbors. Government officials say steadily improving technology has led to cleaner and more efficient operations.

15	apartment complexes	「集合住宅」

It's also made disposal easier for many. At apartment complexes around the country, residents are issued cards to scan every time they drop food waste into a designated bin. The bin weighs what they've dropped in; at the end of the month they get a bill.

Eom Jung-suk, 60, has never been charged more than a dollar for the service. In April, she paid 26 cents. But the monthly bill makes her more aware of how much she throws away.

"Just today, at breakfast, I told my daughters to take just enough to eat," she said.

Notes
1. 韓国料理は量が多いことで有名である．注文した料理の他に，小皿に入った副菜が出てきて無料で自由におかわりができる．客が食べ残すほどの大量の料理でもてなすのが韓国の伝統的流儀で，料理を残すことは「じゅうぶん満足した」という客側の意思表示でもある．
2. 嫌気性消化とは，有機物を微生物の作用によって分解し，バイオガスと有機肥料を生成するプロセス．このプロセスは，酸素の供給が制限された状態，つまり嫌気性条件下で進行する．嫌気性消化は，廃棄物処理，バイオガスの生産，有機廃棄物のリサイクル，エネルギーの生産など，さまざまな分野で使用される．

Post-reading

A: Word Match
Write the appropriate description letter in the empty column next to the compounds.

1.	Potent greenhouse gases		a. Similar systems.
2.	Vast majority		b. A place specifically for separating and disposing of garbage or waste.
3.	Comparable programs		c. The largest number by far.
4.	Culinary tradition		d. A heavy colorless gas used for bubbly drinks, which is a major contributor to climate change.
5.	Mountainous terrain		e. Muddy, slimy, disorganized waste.
6.	Terrible stench		f. The converting of waste, or breakdown of microorganisms, through deprivation of oxygen.
7.	Designated bin		g. Hilly ground.
8.	Processing facility		h. A mechanical or technical method of extracting gases from an enclosed area.
9.	Sludgy mess		i. Something added to animal diets to increase nutritional value.
10.	Climate change		j. The cooking recipes passed down in a culture.
11.	Anaerobic digestion		k. A very bad smell.
12.	Carbon dioxide		l. The heating up of the earth due to emissions of greenhouse gases.
13.	Feed supplement		m. Powerful volatile emissions that contribute to climate change.
14.	Exhaust system		n. A garbage container specifically for a certain kind of waste.

B: Comprehension Questions
1. How many tons of food is thrown away around the world each year and where is it put?
2. What problems does this rotting food cause?
3. Why are governments from around the world studying South Korean facilities for

food waste?
4. How is the South Korean system paid for, and how much does it cost?
5. Why does South Korea's culinary system result in lots of uneaten food?
6. What limits the spread of landfills in South Korea?
7. When did it become illegal to send food waste to landfills?
8. How much does it cost to throw out 20 liters of waste?
9. What happens to the waste?
10. What is leftover from the moisture and the solids and what is it used for?
11. What happens to the 70,000 tons of food waste at the biogas facility in Goyang?
12. What are some problems and complaints about the South Korean system, and what is the government doing to tackle these problems?

C: Discussion Questions
1. What do you think of South Korean's system?
2. In terms of food waste, does Japan's culinary tradition face the same problem as South Korea's?
3. When you were in elementary school, did you ever visit a garbage processing or incinerator sight?
4. Do you know what happens to food waste in Japan?
5. How can we cut down on food waste in our own homes?
6. Do you think the government should enact better laws and improve its waste management system?

D: Research Activities
1. Look up the amount of food waste your country generates each year.
2. What is that per capita?
3. What is Japan's ranking in the world for food waste disposal?
4. What are the main methods of dealing with food waste and solid waste in general?
5. What are the worst countries in the world for waste disposal?
6. What are some solutions for dealing with food waste around the world?

Unit 7
My Frustrating Attempt At a Plastic-Free Day

It's all around us, despite its adverse effects on the planet.
In a 24-hour experiment, one journalist tried to go plastic-free.

Pre-reading

A: Crossword
Match the words in the Word Bank to their descriptions to fill in the crossword.

Word Bank

Absolutist	Absurd	Addicted	Consequence	Disoriented	Disposable
Eco-conscious*	Ephemeral	Hygiene	Intrepid	Invention	Lurking
Motivates	Ordeal	Overwhelmed	Synthetic	Versatile	Violation

*Use hyphen when filling in the crossword.

Across
2. (n.) A severe or difficult experience.
6. (n.) A breaking of a rule. A crime less serious than a felony.
7. (adj.) Awareness of the environment.
8. (adj.) Brave, fearless, audacious, bold.
11. (n.) Effect, outcome, result.
14. (n.) The promotion of cleanliness, especially to prevent illness.
15. (adj.) Transitory, lasting for a very short period of time, a day.
16. (adj.) Can be put down or thrown away.
17. (adj.) Inconsistent with logic or common sense, ridiculous.
18. (adj.) Having great diversity, able to do many things.

Down
1. (n.) A creation of something new resulting from study and experimentation.
3. (v.) Present participle. To lie in, wait, ambush, loiter, behave in a sneaky way.
4. (adj.) To be dependent on something, compulsive use, habitual behavior.
5. (v.) Past participle. To be lost, without sense of direction.
9. (v.) Past participle. To be submerged in emotions, drowned in work, etc.
10. (v.) Propels, inspires, gives incentive for actions.
12. (adj.) Man made, not of natural origin, made by chemical reactions.
13. (n.) One who sticks to one point severely, extremist, a tyrant.

B: Discussion Questions
1. How many objects have you touched or used today that are made of plastic?
2. Do you think you could go through a day without using any plastic?
3. Why is plastic used for so many things? (Why is it good?)
4. Why is plastic bad? What problems does it create?
5. Which countries use the most plastic?
6. Are there any objects that you think could be made without plastic?

C: Reading Graphs, Maps and Statistics
Graph 1:
Per Capita Consumption of Plastics in Kilograms Per Person

1. Which area of the world has the most per capita plastic waste?
2. What rank is Japan in terms of plastic waste per person?
3. How much have people in Japan increased their plastic use since 1980?

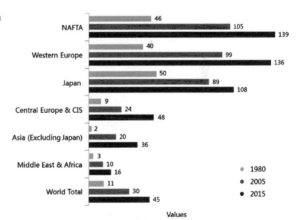

https://www.researchgate.net/figure/Per-capita-consumption-of-plastics-in-kg-person16_fig2_338027440

Graph 2:
Mismanaged Waste in Kilograms Per Person

4. Which area of the world has the least amount of mismanaged (un-recycled) plastic waste?
5. Why is Europe the lowest in graph 2, yet one of the highest users of plastic waste in graph 1?

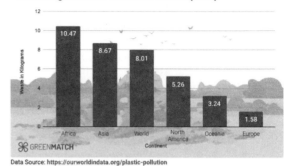

https://www.greenmatch.co.uk/blog/plastic-pollution-facts

By A. J. Jacobs   Jan. 11, 2023

On the morning of the day I had decided to go without using plastic products — or even touching plastic — I opened my eyes and put my bare feet on the carpet. Which is made of nylon, a type of plastic. I was only seconds into my experiment, and I had already committed a violation.

Since its invention more than a century ago, plastic has crept into every aspect of our lives. It's hard to go even a few minutes without touching this durable, lightweight, wildly versatile substance. Plastic has made possible thousands of modern conveniences, but it has come with downsides, especially for the environment.

Last week, in a 24-hour experiment, I tried to live without it to see what plastic stuff we can't do without and what we may be able to give up.

Most mornings I check my iPhone soon after waking up. On the appointed day, this was not possible, given that each iPhone contains plastic. In preparation for the experiment, I had stashed my device in a closet. I quickly found that not having access to it left me feeling disoriented and bold, as if I were some sort of intrepid time traveler.

I made my way toward the bathroom, only to stop myself before I went in. "Could you open the door for me?" I asked my wife, Julie. "The doorknob has a plastic coating." She opened it for me, letting out a "this is going to be a long day" sigh.

My morning hygiene routine needed a total revamp, which required advanced preparations. I could not use my regular toothpaste, toothbrush, shampoo or liquid soap, all of which were encased in plastic or made of plastic.

Fortunately, there is a big industry of plastic-free products targeted at eco-conscious consumers, and I had bought an array of them, a haul that included a bamboo toothbrush with bristles made of wild boar hair.

Instead of toothpaste, I had a jar of gray charcoal-mint toothpaste pellets. I popped one in, chewed it, sipped water and brushed. It was nice and minty. I liked my shampoo bar. A shampoo bar is just what it sounds like: a bar of shampoo.

Before I was done in the bathroom, I had broken the rules a second time, by using the toilet.

Getting dressed was also a challenge, given that so many clothing items include plastic. I chose a pair of old chinos. The tag said "100 percent cotton," but there was plastic lurking in the zipper tape, the internal waistband and woven label.

Happily, my underwear did not represent a plastic violation — blue boxers made of organic cotton with a cotton drawstring in place of the elastic (which is often plastic) waistband.

For my upper body, I lucked out. Our friend Kristen had knitted my wife a sweater for a birthday present. It was 100 percent merino wool. "Could I borrow Kristen's sweater for the day?" I asked Julie. "You're going to stretch it out," Julie said.

Plastics Present and Past

The world produces about 400 million metric tons of plastic waste each year, according to a United Nations report. About half is tossed out after a single use. The report noted that "we have become addicted to single-use plastic products — with severe environmental, social, economic and health consequences."

I estimated that I toss about 800 plastic items in the garbage a year — takeout containers, pens, cups, and more.

Before my Day of No Plastic I called Gabby Salazar, a social scientist who studies what motivates people to support environmental causes, and asked for her advice.

"It might be better to start small," Dr. Salazar said. "Start by creating a single habit — like always carrying a stainless-steel water bottle. After you've got that down, you start another habit, like taking produce bags to the grocery. You build up gradually. Otherwise, you'll just be overwhelmed."

Admittedly, living completely without plastic is probably an absurd idea. Despite its faults, plastic is a crucial ingredient in medical equipment, smoke alarms, helmets and other things. There's truth to the plastics industry's catchphrase from the 1990s:

"Plastics make it possible."

In many cases it can help the environment: Plastic airplane parts are lighter than metal ones, which mean less fuel and lower CO_2 emissions. Solar panels and wind turbines have plastic parts. That said, the world is overloaded with the stuff, especially the disposable forms. The Earth Policy Institute estimates that people go through one trillion single-use plastic bags each year.

There's some debate over when plastic entered the world, but many date it to 1855, when a British metallurgist, Alexander Parkes, patented a thermoplastic material as a waterproof coating for fabrics. Over the decades, labs across the world birthed other types, all with a similar chemistry: They are polymer chains, and most are made from petroleum or natural gas. Thanks to chemical additives, plastics vary wildly. They can be opaque or transparent, stretchy or brittle. They are known by many names, including polyester and Styrofoam, and by shorthand like PVC and PET.

Plastic manufacturing ramped up for World War II and was crucial to the war effort, providing nylon parachutes and Plexiglas aircraft windows. That was followed by a postwar boom, said Susan Freinkel, the author of "Plastic: A Toxic Love Story," a book on the history and science of plastic.

"Plastic went into things like Formica counters, refrigerator liners, car parts, clothing, shoes, just all sorts of stuff that was designed to be used for a while," she said.

Then things took a turn. "Where we really started to get into trouble is when it started going into single-use stuff," Ms. Freinkel said. "I call it prefab litter."

The outpouring of straws, cups, bags and other ephemera has led to disastrous consequences for the environment. According to a study by the Pew Charitable Trusts, more than 11 million metric tons of plastic enter oceans each year, leaching into the water, disrupting the food chain and choking marine life.

Close to one-fifth of plastic waste gets burned, releasing CO_2 into the air, according to the Organization for Economic Cooperation and Development, which says only 9 percent of plastics are recycled.

Plastic may also harm our health. Certain plastic additives — such as BPA and phthalates — may disrupt the endocrine system in humans, according to the National Institute of Environmental Health Sciences. Worrying effects may include behavioral problems and lower testosterone levels in boys and lower thyroid hormone levels and preterm births for women.

"Solving this plastic problem can't fall entirely on the shoulders of consumers," Dr. Salazar told me. "We need to work on it on all fronts."

 It's Everywhere

Early in my no-plastic day, I started to see the world differently. Everything looked menacing, harboring hidden polymers. The kitchen was particularly fraught. Anything I could use for cooking was off-limits — the toaster, the oven, the microwave.

I decided to go foraging for raw food items.

I left my building using the stairs, rather than the elevator with its plastic buttons, and walked to a health food store near our apartment in New York.

When I go shopping, I try to remember to take a cloth bag with me. This time, I had brought along seven bags, all of them cotton. I also had two glass containers.

At the store, I filled up one of my cotton bags with apples and oranges. On close inspection, I noticed that each rind had a sticker with a code. Another likely violation, but I ignored it.

At the bulk bins, I scooped walnuts and oatmeal into my glass dishes using a steel ladle from home. The bins themselves were plastic, which I ignored, because I was hungry.

I went to the cashier. At which point it was time to pay. Which was a problem. Credit cards were out. So was my iPhone's Apple Pay. Paper money was another violation: Although U.S. paper currency is made mainly of cotton and linen, each bill likely contains synthetic fibers.

I had brought along a cotton sack full of coins. Yes, a big old sack heavy with quarters, dimes and pennies — about $60 worth that I had withdrawn from Citibank and my kids' piggy banks.

At the checkout counter, I started stacking coins as quickly as I could between nervous glances at the customers behind me. I counted out $19.02 — exact change! — and went home to eat my breakfast.

A couple of hours later, in search of a plastic-free lunch, I walked to a sandwich shop, toting my rectangular glass dish and bamboo cutlery.

"Can you make the salad in this glass container?" I asked,

holding it up. "One minute please," the man behind the counter said, tersely. He called over a manager, who said OK. Victory! But the manager then rejected my follow-up request to use my steel scooper.

After lunch, I headed to Central Park, figuring that this was a spot in Manhattan where I could relax in a plastic-free environment. I took the subway there, which scored me more violations, since the trains themselves have plastic parts.

At least I didn't sit in one of those plastic orange seats. I had brought my own: an unpainted, fold-up teak chair. I plopped my chair down near a pole in the middle of the car. One guy had a please-don't-talk-to-me look in his eyes, but the other passengers were so buried in their phones that the sight of a man on a wooden chair didn't faze them.

Back home, I recorded some of my impressions. I wrote on paper with an unpainted cedar pencil, by candle light, from a "Zero Waste Pencil tin set" (regular pencils contain plastic-filled yellow paint).

Then I sat there in my wooden chair. Phone-less. Internet-less. Julie took some pity on me and offered to play a game of cards. I shook my head. "Plastic coating," I said.

At 10:30 p.m., exhausted, I lay down on my makeshift bed — cotton sheets on the wood floor, since my mattress and pillows are plasticky.

I woke up the next morning glad to have survived my ordeal and be reunited with my phone — but also with a feeling of defeat.

I had made 164 violations, by my count. As Dr. Salazar had predicted, I felt overwhelmed. And also uncertain. What plastic-free items really made a difference, and what is mere green-washing?

I thought back to something that the author Susan Freinkel had told me: "I'm not an absolutist at all. If you came into my kitchen, you would be like, what the hell? You wrote this book and look at how you live!"

Ms. Freinkel does make an effort, she said. She avoids single-use bags, cups and packaging, among other things. I pledge to try, too.

I'll start with small things, building up habits. I liked the shampoo bar. And I can take produce bags to the grocery. I might even pack my steel water bottle and bamboo cutlery for my lunch.

And I'll proudly wear the "Keep the Sea Plastic Free" T-shirt that I bought online. It's just 10 percent polyester.

28　make a difference「状況を改善する」
　　green-washing「うわべだけの環境保護」
31　what the hell?「いったいどういうこと？」

Notes

1 歯磨きタブレットは従来のチューブ入り歯磨きペーストに代わる固形の歯磨き粉．歯で噛み砕き，水で濡らした歯ブラシで磨く．また，固形シャンプーは液状ではなく石鹸のような固形状のシャンプーで，水で濡らして泡だててから使う．両者ともパッケージにプラスチックを使わなくて済み，成分にもココナツオイルや炭など天然由来の原料が用いられ，添加物を使わないなど環境に優しい．

Post-reading

A: Word Match

Write the appropriate description letter in the empty column next to the compounds.

1. Hygiene routine		a.	People who purchase products that have a minimum negative effect on the environment.
2. Feeling disoriented		b.	Babies who are born before the normally accepted gestation period.
3. Eco-conscious consumers		c.	The amount of the primary male sex hormone and androgen in a person.
4. Waterproof coating		d.	Advertisements or information that make a polluting product seem ecological.
5. Endocrine system		e.	Manmade threads that make up a textile.
6. Testosterone levels		f.	Daily practice of keeping oneself clean.
7. Preterm births		g.	It regulates the body's hormones and all biological processes including aging, brain development and metabolism.
8. Thyroid hormone		h.	Emotionally lost.
9. Synthetic fibers		i.	It controls the body's metabolism, the process in which your body transforms the food we eat into energy.
10. Green-washing		j.	A varnish or resin that covers a surface to prevent it being ruined by rain, or spilled liquids.

B: Comprehension Questions

1. What did the author of the article decide to go without for a day?
2. How long did it take before he committed a violation?
3. What regular daily items could he not use or even touch? Name six.
4. What was his 2nd violation?
5. How many metric tons of plastic waste are produced each year in the world?
6. How many plastic items does the author consider he throws in the garbage each year?
7. What advice does Dr. Salazar offer to tackle their plastic addiction?
8. Why is it absurd to try to live 100% plastic-free?
9. How do some plastics help the environment?
10. When did "we really start to get in trouble" with plastics, according to Ms. Freinkel?
11. How does plastic harm our health?

12. How many violations had the author made at the end of his 24 hour experiment?

C: Discussion Questions
1. Do you think you could cut plastic out of your life?
2. What kinds of plastics can you reduce or stop using?
3. What can we use instead of plastic?
4. Have you ever seen plastic waste on the beach, or streets and rivers in your country?
5. How did this make you feel?
6. How can individuals make a difference?
7. Do you support laws to curb plastic use?

D: Research Activities
1. How many tons of plastic were produced in 1950, 1980 and in 2020?
2. What are the top 5 countries for plastic pollution in the world?
3. What are the top 5 recycling countries in the world?
4. How much plastic is found in the North Pacific, North Atlantic and Indian Oceans?
5. What are the main kinds of plastic waste? (e.g. pet bottles, pens, tooth brushes etc.)
6. What are alternatives to plastic bags, toothbrushes, pens, straws etc.?

テキストの音声は、弊社 HP　https://www.eihosha.co.jp/
の「テキスト音声ダウンロード」のバナーからダウンロードできます。
また、下記 QR コードを読み込み、音声ファイルをダウンロードするか、
ストリーミングページにジャンプして音声を聴くことができます。

表紙デザイン：山本　彩

Changes and Choices
with articles from The New York Times
現代諸相 ニューヨークタイムズ

2025 年 2 月 28 日　初　版

編 注 者　　喜　多　留　女
　　　　　　K. W. Adams

発 行 者　　佐 々 木　　元

発 行 所　株式会社　英　宝　社
〒101-0032 東京都千代田区岩本町 2-7-7
TEL 03 (5833) 5870　　FAX 03 (5833) 5872
https://www.eihosha.co.jp/

ISBN 978-4-269-19045-0 C1082

［製版：伊谷企画／印刷・製本：モリモト印刷株式会社］

本テキストの一部または全部を、コピー、スキャン、
デジタル化等での無断複写・複製は、著作権法上での
例外を除き禁じられています。本テキストを代行業者
等の第三者に依頼してのスキャンやデジタル化はたと
え個人や家庭内での利用であっても著作権侵害となり、
著作権法上一切認められておりません。